ROJIN,
BUDDHA'S
MYSTICAL POWER

IRH Press

BOOKS
IRH PRESS
New York

ISBN 13: 978-1-942125-82-2
ISBN 10: 1-942125-82-8

Printed in Canada

First Edition

Cover/Interior Image: © homydesign/shutterstock.com
artida/shutterstock.com

漏尽
通力

ROJIN,

BUDDHA'S
MYSTICAL POWER

Its Ultimate Attainment
in Today's World

RYUHO OKAWA

IRH Press

Contents

Chapter 1

A Spiritual View of Life

Chapter 2

Theories of Spiritual Phenomena

Chapter 3
Different Kinds of Spiritual Ability

Chapter 4
Rojin, the Mystical Power

Chapter 5

Buddha's Truth and Its Study

Chapter 6

Serenity Within and Prayer

Chapter 7

Lecture on *Rojin*, Buddha's Mystical Power

PREFACE TO THE NEW
AND REVISED EDITION

Over three decades ago, at the age of thirty-one, the author wrote the original edition of this book after completing the basic trilogy of *The Laws of the Sun*, *The Golden Laws*, and *The Laws of Eternity*. In fact, this book was so much ahead of its time that it was kept out of print for a time.

However, nowadays a book that refers to various aspects of advanced psychic abilities would be extremely valuable, so I thought it should be reprinted in a new and revised edition. Another reason was that there have also been those who have disrespected sacred spiritual messages.

According to traditional interpretation, *rojin*, the mystical power, is one of the six divine powers. It has been considered the power to overcome and vanquish worldly delusions. The word "*ro*" refers to worldly delusions and desires ["*jin*" means to vanquish them]. There are also the terms "*uro*" [being bound by worldly delusions] and "*muro*" [being free from worldly delusions] in Buddhism.

It is said that when Shakyamuni attained enlightenment under the Bodhi tree, he also gained three insights, one of which was *rojin*. At that time, Shakyamuni Buddha decided to end the austerity of fasting and enter the Middle Way. He then accepted an offering of milk porridge from the village girl Sujata.

From this, it can be understood that the mystical power of *rojin* was not about eliminating worldly desires altogether, but about being able to use exceptional psychic abilities without being swayed by worldly desires. In this way, *rojin* is compatible with the perspectives of wisdom and "One who understands the world" which is one of the ten titles of the Buddha. This is a new theory by the authentic Buddha.

I would also like to point out that a prior lecture regarding the original edition has been added as Chapter 7 in this new and revised edition.

Ryuho Okawa
Master & CEO of Happy Science Group
April 10, 2020

PREFACE

This book, *Rojin, Buddha's Mystical Power – Its Ultimate Attainment in Today's World*, discusses various types of spiritual abilities. Of these, special consideration is given in explaining what the ultimate attainment of spiritual or psychic ability in today's world would be, and what the state of an ultimate psychic individual would be like. Shakyamuni Buddha possessed six divine powers, standing out significantly among other major religious teachers of the past by achieving the highest level of *rojin*, the mystical power.

Traditionally, *rojin* is considered the ability to overcome and vanquish worldly desires, but it can be misinterpreted as a recommendation to leave this world to enter nirvana. I think of *rojin* as the ability to live a spiritual life while still on earth, a life like a sharp Japanese sword that keeps its luster without rusting.

From another perspective, it is the ability to live a completely normal life while having immense psychic abilities; it is the ability to actualize the extraordinary in the ordinary.

I believe that the state of *rojin* is the golden key to open the way to consider what enlightenment would be for people living today. From this point of view, I believe this book to be a must-read for seekers of Truth.

> *Ryuho Okawa*
> *Master & CEO of Happy Science Group*
> *March 1988*

Chapter 1

A Spiritual View
of Life

1

Turning Point in Life

Every person constantly searches for purpose in life, and in the course of our lives, we will come across various kinds of turning points.

Among them, the most significant would be the turning point of religious encounters. What exactly would be a religious encounter? It is to have contact or be confronted by something that is beyond this world on earth.

Indeed, no matter who you are, you will necessarily experience various kinds of turning points in life.

One example of a turning point could be if you had fallen ill in childhood. It could be the death of a parent, or the separation of your parents, or something of similar nature.

In elementary school, you may have been bullied. In junior high school, you may have experienced setbacks in club activities, or in high school, you may have worried over your future education.

Upon graduating from high school, students might often have a hard time deciding whether to get a job or go to college. If they choose to go to college, they may have difficulty choosing which school to attend. In many cases, they may not make it into their first choice, and they would have to attend a school they had not intended to enter.

In addition, they may have difficulty in keeping up with their studies after entering university, or they may have to repeat classes or even drop out.

When it comes to finding a job, it is just like the situation of higher education. It is quite difficult to get your first choice job; when you go for job interviews, you may pass the first or second screening but fail the third.

Even if you managed to join a company that meets your expectations, there are often many stumbling blocks awaiting you. Your peers may get promoted ahead of you, you may unwittingly make mistakes in your job, or you may fall ill as a result of overwork.

Someone who is well-qualified and initially expected to advance may fail unexpectedly; they may be demoted and drop out of contention for the best jobs.

There are also times when those who were formerly unnoticed may gain the ability and become unexpectedly qualified to emerge as your rivals and move up the ladder of job positions. Your junior associate could become your boss. You may experience such a blow in your career.

In addition to career issues, there is also the personal issue of marriage. Marriage can be considered a challenge, and it is one of the major experiences in one's life. As with the choice of one's job, the choice of one's spouse is very important.

It is said that there are three major trials in life, namely education, employment, and marriage.

The majority of readers of this book will have already experienced the trial of obtaining higher education. Those who are not currently students would have probably gone through the challenge of finding employment. And I believe that some of you might experience problems concerning the issue of marriage.

When deciding who to choose as a spouse, people experience a lot of problems.

There are various marriage consultancy services in the world, and they may act as a go-between to explain the requirements of both parties.

When a man wishes to meet a woman, he may have certain requirements such as having good looks, holding at least a junior college degree, having healthy parents, not being an only daughter, and so on. He may add other preferences such as having a good personality, being a devoted person, being a good cook, or having good homemaking skills.

On the other hand, when a woman seeks a potential mate, she too may have requirements for a husband, such as having an annual income above a certain level, being a second or a third son so he could therefore live apart from his parents, being at least 170 centimeters tall, not weighing more than a certain number of kilograms, and so on.

Even in such cases, while making various choices concerning worldly situations, people may somehow receive some indication of divine fate or influence from the realm beyond this world. Specifically, they may expect help from their own guardian and guiding spirits, or believe in some kind of divine connection that had existed before being born into this world.

Many people do not usually think about God, Buddha, or spiritual things, yet when they are faced with turning points such as choosing a school, getting a job, or getting married, they may feel the presence of something spiritual.

When it comes to marriage, we hear people speak of destined soul mates. Many young women seem to believe such stories and they tend to think that more than 80% or 90% of people should be divinely matched. This would indicate that marriage is a cue that encourages one to gain a spiritual outlook on life.

After marriage, having children may cause you to feel mystically affected. A child is not something that you can have at will, and when you realize you are going to have a baby, you will have a mysterious feeling that you have been given a child.

Some people may experience divorce, or some may suffer bereavement from the death of the spouse.

In the course of our lives, we experience many different turning points. Basically, these turning points present us with options to choose from. "Should I go to the right or left, or should I go straight ahead or retreat?" There will always be turning points like this.

These are the circumstances not just for a selected few. Every person encounters many turning points again and again in their lives. Depending on which choices one makes at any given time, one's life can greatly change, and you will notice this when you look back on your own life.

It is like walking through a maze. If you make a mistake when choosing whether to turn right or left, you will never manage to get out, but if you make a good choice, you will be able to get out of the maze. Thus, in the end, your life can be changed by your decision of which direction to turn.

At such turning points in life, people tend to rely on things that are mysterious in nature, such as divination, onomancy, fortune telling, or astrology. They try to seek answers from practices that profess to go beyond normal human knowledge.

For example, when it comes to the matter of marriage, there are times when one wavers in deciding whether to marry A or B. At such times, one may go to see a fortune teller who can determine which potential partner has a closer spiritual bond, or if the choice of the other would cause some failure. Then, this marriage seeker, in following such advice, may experience even more confusion. There are many cases like this.

In the end, we try to figure out the guidelines on our own, but also hope that there might be some way to see one step further. This is because, after all, no one wants to fail.

It is hard for a person to foresee what will happen six months, one year, three years, five years, or ten years later. Because we cannot tell the future and because it belongs in the realm beyond our perception, we wonder if we might obtain some help from something greater, beyond human knowledge.

I believe that these turning points in our lives are opportunities for us to awaken to a spiritual view of life. That is how I see it.

2

Awakening to Spirituality

As you face the turning points in life, you are made aware of awakening to spirituality.

In dealing with turning points in their lives, many people are attracted to fortune telling or divination and seek matches made in heaven or by destiny. But these attractions are temporary, used only to make random decisions at the given moment. As the saying goes, "Danger past, and God forgotten"; after a problem is dealt with they usually forget about matters beyond this world.

For example, after getting married, people may easily forget about having sacred feelings of Divinity as they go back to their mundane daily lives, even though they had seriously considered the choice and had earnestly sought God or Buddha for help.

From the perspective of the other world, the guardian spirits make much effort, struggling to guide those facing times of trial on earth. There are countless instances when the guardian spirits feel disappointed when those on earth are so ungrateful, totally forgetting to give thanks for the efforts made by the guardian spirits as they return to their easy lives.

Your life is not the result of only the choices you make; there are many unseen forces at work.

Usually, people have a guardian spirit that works day and night to guide them in a good direction.

For major problems that are beyond the control of a guardian spirit, there is a guiding spirit that can provide constant advice. Those who have notable professions in this world always have a guiding spirit to give them advice.

However, most people completely forget to be thankful to them and live a life without gratitude. Instead, they may just think, "I was lucky" or "I was unlucky," or "My success was totally due to my having better talent and capabilities."

Thus, many people are slow to awaken to spirituality, even though they have chances to do so at turning points in their lives.

I observe that one characteristic of these people is a strong ego. They regard themselves as superior, are narcissistic, and make self-benefit their priority. In short, they are self-absorbed.

The truth is that there are invisible threads that extend from the spiritual world, beyond perception; they are being pulled to guide us in various ways, but we usually do not feel the tug of the guidance and think that we have achieved everything on our own. On the other hand, when we make a mistake, we tend to blame something or someone other than ourselves for the failure. This is how we tend to think. You could say that it is a self-centered way of life.

However, if you are truly prepared to humble yourself before God or Buddha, or before high spirits, you will inevitably be obliged to experience a great awakening to spirituality.

There are two ways to be awakened to spirituality.

The first case is when a setback prompts you to seek God or Buddha. With the desire to get back on your feet, you look for a solution, and may eventually turn to God or Buddha, or join a religious group. This is one way to be awakened to spirituality.

One of the most conspicuous occurrences is that the media often features the harm caused by religions, or it focuses on religious groups' problems, but it is also true that religion provides refuge for people in difficulty.

There are people who have been hurt in the social sphere or their workplaces. Where should they turn? People may suffer from broken marriages. Where can they go? A mother may experience issues raising her children. Where can she go? Where should the unemployed go? Where should those suffering from illness go? There are people who suffer from various other problems in life. Where can they turn?

Many of these people do not have any place to go for solace. For those people who are suffering, the entrance to religion can open to provide them with guidance. In this sense, it is true that religions serve the role of a hospital, and in a larger sense accommodate people as a sanctuary, in spite of all the negative comments on their reputation. This is a role that religion can play.

Then there is also a completely different perspective. It is one for people who have achieved success in situations one after another, people who have had a lot of luck when things have gone as planned and readily climbed their way to accomplishment. These people are also very often blessed by God. Actually, these outcomes are most often due to their faith.

It is not uncommon for noted business leaders to practice nightly meditation while seated on the floor, receiving inspiration from which they might make important business decisions.

It is also true that the more accomplished a person is, the greater the importance he or she places on spiritual intuition. This is what is called an inspired hunch. People with successful experiences have often received such spiritual help at some point in their lives. There are many instances that some intuition, instinct, or inspiration has led them to great success in business.

Some people have received inspiration that led them to create new inventions and achieve great success, while others have averted critical situations based on intuition.

There was a global stock market crash last autumn [in 1987], but some people seemed to have been able to foresee it intuitively, leading them to sell their stock holdings beforehand. They must have perceived some kind of guidance.

As you can see, I believe that there will always be clues for spiritual awakening, both in times of setbacks as well as in times of success. Indeed, you can find meaning in living this life on earth.

In this life, it is prearranged that people undergo spiritual discipline. It is because deep down we place great importance on knowing more about spiritual things that cannot be seen, heard, or felt in this world. It is because we have great respect for being awakened to the world beyond earthly understanding.

Therefore, I ask myself, "Doesn't the experience of awakening to spirituality in our life on earth represent one of our greatest advancements? Doesn't it also provide the opportunity to discover the meaning of one's life in this incarnation?"

3

Material Things and Temptation

There is another issue to consider. Even for those who have experienced a spiritual awakening, life in this world involves a very difficult problem: It is how to deal with material things. As we live on earth, our minds are inevitably caught up with things of material nature.

The "materials" in question can be expressed as objects, goods, or things that are obtained by wealth. We will become obsessed with these things. Typical examples of material things are money, houses, cars, fine clothes, and luxury items such as jewelry or expensive adornments.

In addition, the opposite sex is sometimes referred to as a presence that arouses desire; therefore, in this way it is considered to be similar to material objects. It is said that the greatest hindrance to spiritual awakening is materialistic temptation, and materialistic temptation includes not only valuables but also the attraction of the opposite sex, especially beautiful women when regarding men.

In response to this outlook, some people might argue that it is problematic to view the existence of the opposite sex as a temptation since men and women have been created by God.

However, there have been factual examples in the past where the presence of the opposite sex or material goods were obstacles to spiritual awakening. So the important theme here is how to think about and deal with the issue of material things.

It is this problem of material things and temptation that has troubled religious leaders and practitioners in the past.

Even Jesus Christ was troubled by this temptation. As you can see from the Bible, he was subjected to temptation in the wilderness for forty days and forty nights.

Jesus was tempted in various ways by Beelzebub, leader of Satanic demons. In one instance, the tempter said to him, "If you are the Son of God, command these stones to become loaves of bread." Responding to this, Jesus said, "Man shall not live by bread alone."

Then the devil took him to the holy city [Jerusalem] and set him on the pinnacle of the temple and said to him, "If you are the Son of God, throw yourself down."

The reason why Satan tested him in this way was that there is a passage in the Old Testament that goes, "He [God] will command his angels concerning you," and "On their hands they will bear you up, lest you strike your foot against a stone." So Satan urged Jesus to jump off the pinnacle, saying that if he were the Son of God, angels would surely come to his rescue. He tried to tempt Jesus' ego.

Then Jesus replied, "Again it is written, 'You shall not put the Lord your God to the test.'"

The devil's temptations of Jesus actually occurred, showing that Jesus was also subjected to temptations as he lived as a human being. The bread may have symbolized food, the temptation to eat. Also, jumping off the pinnacle of the temple may have symbolized personal honor.

Satan also said to Jesus, "All these I will give you, if you will fall down and worship me," showing him all the kingdoms of the world and their glory. But Jesus repelled him, saying, "Be gone, Satan!"

With such worldly desires, Satan tried to tempt a holy person. There have been many cases like this.

These types of situations have always occurred, and saints have always rebuffed such temptations. The reason why they occur is to teach people on earth who are swayed by material things, to show them how to overcome temptations and instead live truthful lives as humanly as possible.

It was not only the case of Jesus. The same held for Shakyamuni Buddha; it is well known that he lived in luxury in Kapilavastu until the age of twenty-nine years old. He was raised as a prince, had many servants to fulfill his wishes, ate sumptuous food, and had retainers to accompany him wherever he went.

He also had a number of beautiful consorts to attend him from the time of his teens; it seems that he had four or five of them. Among them was the famous Yashodhara, but there were also others. Even though these were arrangements made by his father the king, he most probably would have had days of pleasure during the dozen years or so with such women.

However, amid this luxurious lifestyle, he suffered because of attachments, which caused him to think, "This cannot be the true way of human life. If I can break free from attachments, I will surely achieve true enlightenment. Something is wrong with this way of life."

We have seen the examples of Jesus and Shakyamuni Buddha in the past. On the other hand, those who can be called "saints" in the modern age do not seem to totally deny material things or the opposite sex.

The same is true for religious teachers born in modern Japan. Kanzo Uchimura, author and Christian evangelist, for example, had a wife and held regular jobs. Masaharu Taniguchi, New Thought leader and founder of Seicho-no-Ie, also had a wife, held a job, and had worldly wealth. There has also been another religious leader who was married, supported his family, and engaged in profitable business activities in addition to preaching his religious beliefs.

In the past, saintly persons seemed to have rejected material things, adopting the attitude of living only for spiritual purposes. More recently, viewing the activities of religious people in modern times, we can see that they are moving in the direction of seeking a path based on integrating the realms of the material and spiritual, rather than simply keeping the two realms separate.

If we simply rejected material things and only sought things that were spiritual, then there would be no meaning to this three-dimensional existence. If we assume that this world on earth is only temporary, and therefore meaningless and instead filled with suffering, as the true world exists outside of this three-dimensional world, then wouldn't it have been a mistake to have been born in this world in the first place?

If that is the case, then wouldn't the greatest ideal be to break free from the karma of reincarnation? If to be reincarnated in this world means to be born into a world of suffering, then our greatest joy would be to never be reborn. Therefore, wouldn't the greatest happiness be to transcend the cycles of reincarnation?

In other words, wouldn't the main purpose of spiritual discipline be to become a tathagata by liberating oneself from such cycles?

This way of thinking was included in the early teachings of Buddhism. The spiritual discipline of its practitioners purposefully focused on breaking free from reincarnating into this world, to do without any more suffering.

However, from our current perspective, I can say that this way of thinking only represents one side of Buddha's Truth, not its entirety.

At Happy Science, I clearly teach that spiritual beings draw up plans in the other world before being born into this world. It is not by chance that a human being is born into this world. Human beings are not born by chance, being "thrown into this world" as existentialist philosophy would have it. Nor were they born into a family by chance. In order to be born, it is necessary to create a plan beforehand.

So why are we born into this world on earth?

The answer is that we come into this earthly world for the purpose of soul training and living together with many others to create a utopia. In the process of building a utopia on earth, we will improve ourselves and experience joy in our souls as we grow and share our experiences with peers.

Isn't this what the meaning of this world is all about?

In this perspective, material things can be seen as building blocks that serve to create a utopia on earth. The same can be said of the existence of members of the opposite sex. They also serve to enable the construction of a utopia. These are possible ways to look at life on earth.

If we do not give serious consideration to the previous world, where we existed before being born into this world, and only regard this world negatively as one of suffering and full of attachment, then escaping from attachment would give the greatest meaning to our lives. However, if we understand that we are born into this world on earth with a purpose but only focus on escaping from it, this would mean that we are partially blinded to the truth.

If we can live a wonderful life in this world that corresponds to the realm we want to attain in the afterlife, then by living a heavenly life on earth, the heavenly realm would await us in the afterlife. Thus, it would be aligned with having the goal of a heavenly afterlife and there would not be any cause of a major problem.

This idea would definitely be different from having faith in Amitabha Buddha, in which people only wish for happiness in the afterlife.

A modern way to view the matter of material objects and temptation would be to consider their purpose as serving as building blocks for creating a utopia on earth.

The same perspective can be applied to wealth. Wealth can be a very powerful tool if it is applied effectively to build a utopia. However, if it is used to interfere with the objectives of utopia, it will be very harmful. If someone with abundant financial resources tried to hinder the spreading of Buddha's Truth, this would cause great negative pressure. On the other hand, if such a wealthy person was willing to help spread the Truth, his or her financial power would be greatly effective.

The same can be said of the members of the opposite sex. Carnal desire has been seen as a type of attachment from ancient times, but if a husband and a wife work together to contribute to spreading the Truth or constructing a utopia, the power of the couple will be two, three, or four times greater than each of their individual abilities.

On the other hand, if the husband and wife grow apart from each other, pulling one another down, or opposing and hindering the other from seeking for Buddha's Truth, then the power of each of them would be reduced to one-half or one-third.

Therefore, it is necessary to reconsider how material things and temptation could be interpreted from the perspective of building utopia. In this way, we would be able to find a path to enlightenment in what we used to think of merely as sources of suffering and attachment.

One of the Buddhist sutras that the famous Japanese priest Kukai brought back from Tang Dynasty China was Rishushakukyo [the Principle of Wisdom Sutra]. This sutra includes passages stating that carnal desire leads to the state of the bodhisattva. As the content of the sutra was considered controversial, the teaching was not disseminated to the general public, but only kept within a circle of limited specialists. This was the reason why Esoteric Buddhism received the descriptive term "esoteric."

There is room for dangerous misunderstanding. Some people may think, "If carnal desire leads to the state of the bodhisattva, then everyone should be free to indulge as they wish with the opposite sex and still can become a bodhisattva; then there would be nothing better." However, this way of thinking is a mistake.

From the perspective of truthful utopia, you should think that the emergent desire for utopia can be found in the love between lovers, or between husband and wife. This is the true meaning of the phrase, "carnal desire can lead to the state of the bodhisattva."

If we think of carnal desire merely as a sin or evil, it would be fettered thinking, but the seeds of Buddha's Truth can be found in it. In truth, seeds or sprouts of Buddha's Truth exist in what is called material things and temptation, but they are aspects that should only be considered from the perspective of building utopia on earth.

I think this way of thinking is very important in the modern world.

4

The Path toward Buddha's Truth

After covering the themes of the turning points in life, awakening to spirituality, and dealing with material things and temptation, I would now like to consider the question of how we should enter the path toward Buddha's Truth.

I believe that the most important thing when entering the path toward Buddha's Truth is to have a good mentor or teacher.

There must be many people who wish to seek the Truth or learn more about it, but unfortunately, they are not blessed with good mentors who can guide them. Many people in the world are seeking the path, but the biggest problem is that they cannot find a true teacher.

So how does one find a true teacher?

Many people flutter from one religion to another and their spiritual condition gets worse, not better. Also, problems are common among those who receive negative spiritual influences, causing them to go astray after becoming involved with questionable religious groups.

In those situations, family members and relatives will naturally become opposed to religious activities. They would question dubious religious gatherings, attributing any kind of misfortune to their family member's involvement in such groups.

Therefore, when thinking about the path toward Buddha's Truth, I believe that it is essential to have a good teacher who can give guidance.

Where there is a good teacher, there will be good teaching. Likewise, where there is excellent teaching, there will be excellent results. The existence of a good teacher who gives excellent teachings will necessarily lead people on higher paths of human perfection. These are all essential.

Thus, a good teacher, good teaching, good effects, and good results are needed; these elements have to exist to pave the path, a wonderful path.

It is very important for there to be many people who are willing to become good mentors to others. I feel that we must produce many excellent mentors of Buddha's Truth.

Moreover, it is essential to make available a variety of good teachings for those mentors to use as teaching materials. And if there are a good number of excellent teachings made available, the next step would be how to learn them and put them into practice.

Using the title Happy Science, I started a movement to bring happiness to the whole of humanity; basic to this movement is my desire to produce good mentors who can lead people.

Therefore, I believe that it is necessary to ensure the objectivity and diversity of Buddha's Truth in the textbook form to train people to become excellent mentors; there is an urgent need to establish methodologies for teaching and learning the Truth. Even if there are excellent teachings of Buddha's Truth, they will not result in any beneficial outcome unless people know how to study them.

As for learning Buddha's Truth, methodologies have not yet been firmly established.

For example, since ancient times, it has not been clear how one could achieve enlightenment. This led some believers to develop the practice of the Thousand-day Circumambulation, thinking that all one had to do was walk in the mountains for 1,000 days. Others thought that it would be sufficient to practice *zazen*, sitting in meditation.

There are still others who have believed that fasting or abstaining from material things and attachments was all that was needed, ridding oneself of all earthly ties, or that practicing austerity under a waterfall for purification was all that was necessary.

As you can see, there are many different ways of thinking, and although they embody a part of the religious spirit in one way or another, they have deviated from the main purpose of learning Buddha's Truth.

There is also the formalism of learning Buddha's Truth that advocates the simple chanting of certain Buddhist scriptures even if one does not understand the meaning of their content. There are several sutras that believers still chant. Others may say, "Just copying the scriptures by hand is rewarding, and if you make copies of tens of thousands of scriptures, it will bring you happiness," while others state that "All you have to do is change your name" or "Donate to a shrine, and you will be saved."

Thus, since the method of learning Buddha's Truth has not been firmly established, the wide spread of many different methodologies has made some people follow misguided ideas.

I believe the first step on the path toward Buddha's Truth is to firmly establish an intellectual foundation. I think it is necessary to establish Buddha's Truth in the form of textbooks and teaching materials. They should serve as materials for learning, giving explanations that are objective and universal.

Without these instruments, people who hold common beliefs grounded in this earthly world would have difficulty learning the Truth in a rightful manner. If they cannot achieve enlightenment without becoming completely immersed in the disciplines of the world beyond this, people will most likely be completely unqualified for salvation. This is how it seems to me.

Therefore, it is important to create the substance of Buddha's Truth, which can convince even those people who hold the common beliefs of this world. I think it is also important to establish a methodology for learning and studying the Truth from an intellectual perspective. In this sense, I think we may need to introduce methods that emulate the educational systems used in schools.

5

Aspiration for Enlightenment

To conclude this chapter, I would like to talk about having the aspiration for enlightenment. The foundation of one's spiritual perspective of life is ultimately one's aspiration for enlightenment. It is the mind that seeks enlightenment, or the desire to seek enlightenment.

I would like you to ponder if aspiration is something that can be acquired. I am sure that in every region and all cultures the desire to seek enlightenment can be found.

Such aspiration does not necessarily mean Buddhist enlightenment, but what lies behind the aspiration is the desire to improve, the desire to get closer to God, and it would be something that is inherent in each and every soul.

If the desire to degrade oneself were inherent in the human soul, then our future would be troubled. However, all human beings have the desire to be better. There is much evidence to prove this.

For example, every person seeks the approval of others. It is easy to call this a desire for self-preservation or a craving for honor, and I think that such a desire cannot be flatly denied. We all want to be appreciated by others. No one is happy when others speak ill of them. We all want others to think well of us.

This human tendency works as a kind of bulwark to protect society. For example, please consider the following. If there were a society full of people who wanted to be held in low esteem, it would be a distressed society. However, no matter how evil people may appear to be or how perverse they may seem, they do not want to be spoken ill of by others even though they may malign others.

This tendency works to keep human beings in check. In other words, the desire to improve is embedded in the human mind. You must know that the desire for spiritual improvement, for enlightenment, is one of the innate functions of the soul.

If such a desire lies deep within each soul, then it is important to help and support people to find good qualities within themselves.

How should we help develop the seeds of enlightenment? How should we water and foster their growth? I think these are important questions to ask ourselves.

How could we help nurture the seeds of enlightenment? Ultimately, the important thing would be to show how wonderful it would be to attain enlightenment. However, if what is commonly referred to as "being enlightened" only produces odd people who cannot adapt to society, that would not be the way to justify "enlightenment."

What happens to people when they attain enlightenment, the result of thoroughly exploring their aspiration to be better, which lies deep inside them? If the effect of attaining enlightenment is simply to break free of the evil cycle of reincarnation as I mentioned earlier, then there is no need to be born in this world.

In fact, this would not be the consequence. There must be some more positive significance to enlightenment. We must seek it out. What would this positive significance be? It is, finally, that all people who are spiritually awakened and have a spiritual outlook on life become outstanding and successful in this world, too. The more enlightened a person becomes, the more influential that person should also become in this world.

This will be the focus, the main theme of this book, *Rojin, Buddha's Mystical Power*. I will discuss this in more detail in due course, but simply put, the idea of *rojin*, the mystical power, that I am going to teach at this time can be described as the mystical power of people who have advanced to high levels of spiritual ability while simultaneously honing their skills to be better in this world. This is how I describe *rojin*.

From now on, it will be important to produce people having both otherworldly abilities and the abilities of this world. I believe that such people will exemplify the necessity of having an aspiration for enlightenment.

If Jesus Christ or Shakyamuni Buddha were present on earth today, they would both be proving themselves in the performance of their work as individuals with excellent abilities. Essentially, an enlightened person must become a person with outstanding abilities. I believe that people in the world would not trust the behavior of those who claim to have been spiritually enlightened but whose other abilities are actually questionable.

Therefore, as long as we emphasize the aspiration for enlightenment, we must be able to explain what can be expected as the result of attaining enlightenment. And if enlightenment is something wonderful, if it is a truly worthy goal for a person to pursue, it would not be harmful to show how important the aspiration for enlightenment is.

Therefore, I strongly believe that it is important to incorporate the aspiration for enlightenment as the fundamental idea of our spiritual view of life. Based on this firm basis, we should proceed to explore what awaits us.

Chapter 2

Theories of Spiritual Phenomena

1

Mysteries of the Mind

In this chapter, I would like to consider the phenomena of spiritual pathways.

Let me first begin with the mysteries of the mind. There is much that is unknown about the human mind. It has been described in various ways over the long history of time, and there have been many concepts to explain its workings. However, I do not think there are many people who have been successful in explaining in detail what the mind really is.

As you read this book, if asked to define what your mind really is, I suspect that hardly anyone would have an immediate answer. Perhaps a Zen monk would reply with words that are quite confusing to the question, "What is the mind?" but I do not think that kind of answer would help in understanding the question at all.

The mind is a term that has been familiar to people since ancient times, but unfortunately, we have not been able to understand what it really is.

In considering the mind, let us look at the example of a man who has been given a key to a storehouse of treasure in his backyard but lives without fully understanding what the function of the key is.

He thinks, "I have two house keys, one for my front door and one to enter through the kitchen; I also have another key but I have no idea what it is for." He does not know what the third key is used for and just neglects it, only using the keys to the front door and the kitchen. He never thinks about what the other key is for, never paying attention to it.

It just so happens that there is a building in his backyard. It is a kind of storehouse, but since his parents passed away early on, he was never told what the key was for. So even if he possesses the key, he has no idea what it would open.

In this way, although there is a proper key for the storehouse, he does not understand the relationship between the two, nor does he try to find what the key unlocks.

This is how the majority of people would appear.

However, at some point, possibly on a free Sunday, he happens to be in a curious mood and feels like taking a look in the storehouse in the backyard. "Could it be that key I have that can open it?" He tries the key in the lock, and surprisingly he is able to open the storehouse. Wondering what he might find inside, he gropes his way through the darkness.

To his surprise, he finds a mountain of gold, silver, and precious stones. He is totally astonished.

He thinks to himself: "I have known for all my life that this storehouse existed, but I never imagined that such treasures were inside. I thought it was just a shed or abandoned shack, but in fact, there was an abundance of treasures hidden within. For all these years I have been toiling at my job to earn a living, without ever knowing about the secret treasure."

This is how a person comes to discover themself.

I am speaking metaphorically, but this is a very common occurrence. There are many people who have such keys in their possession for decades without realizing that they are keys to a storehouse they can access.

It is evident that many people have a lot of abilities and qualities, but they pass them by without realizing them.

The mind is just like this storehouse of treasure. The truth is that once you become aware of the access to the secret treasures, you will find unlimited power within you, but for those who do not explore deeply, the door to the storehouse will never open.

As you explore the mysteries of the mind, you will realize how much power is hidden within the human mind.

There are two aspects to the great secrets of the mind.

The first is the secret that we can control what we think. We can actually take control of our thoughts.

However, the majority of people do not realize this. Instead, they normally do not take notice of their thoughts, as if they are like waves that constantly come in and go out on the shore. Thoughts can be described like this.

When we carefully become aware of our thoughts, they can be seen as the constant flow of a river from its source to its rush to the sea. The mind is a powerful thing when it is pointed in a certain direction.

With waves simply lapping against a beach, it would be difficult to generate power from them, but the vigorously flowing water of a river can be stored in a dam to generate hydroelectric power. In this way, if the water is given a particular direction, it can generate power and can be used for a beneficial purpose.

In the same way, when we explore the mind, focusing on how to control thoughts, we can find unexpected power. It may be related to self-realization. If thoughts are focused in a certain direction and sustained for a certain period of time, they can bring surprising results. The power of thoughts can be seen to indicate one aspect of the secrets of the mind.

Regarding the secrets of the mind, there is another aspect to it that is deeper.

In psychology, this part is called the "deep psyche." In religious terms, it can be called "the world of guardian and guiding spirits," or "the world of spirits." There exists a part of the mind that is connected to such a world.

I think most people may have some vague sense of this nature of the mind, or instinctively feel its existence, but they are not usually able to fully comprehend it.

Therefore, by knowing the existence of abundant treasures hidden within the mind, we should be able to forge ahead and explore this infinite world.

These are two aspects related to the mysteries of the mind. The first is that we can exert great power through the control of our thoughts; the second is that when we delve to the bottom of our thoughts and go beyond, we can communicate with the infinite world, the world of the deep psyche, or the Spirit World.

2

Clouding over the Thought Tape

After describing these mysteries of the mind I ask you, what does the human mind look like from the spiritual perspective? The mind can be divided into two parts: surface consciousness and the subconscious. In the middle or border zone between the surface consciousness and the subconscious, there is something called "thought tape."

On this thought tape, there are fields where memories of all sorts are stored. All the memories of things one has thought and done while alive are stored on the thought tape. It is similar to a kind of magnetic tape, an instrument for storing memories. On this instrument, all one's memories are recorded and thoughts are accumulated.

The area where the thought tape is situated separates the surface consciousness from the subconscious. This can be likened to the skull that separates the brain from the scalp. The thought tape can also be described as a kind of membrane that separates the two parts of the mind.

What kinds of things would be found on the thought tape? They would be something like the residue of all of one's thoughts that have been accumulated over one's entire life.

During any given day, you might think of quite a few things. The number of thoughts that come and go in your mind could amount to thousands or tens of thousands. All of these thoughts are stored as if recorded on a tape recorder.

If a thought is of a bad nature, it will produce a cloud on the thought tape, which is originally colorless and transparent. But when any kind of thought becomes imprinted on it, it starts to show color. When one starts to think bad thoughts, the surface of this tape becomes smeared with a variety of spots and stains. Like transparent glass becomes smudged by the touch of any color, the tape becomes less transparent.

This is the characteristic of the majority of people. After being born into this world, the clear glass of their minds becomes clouded by the various effects of education, habits, ideas, and opinions of others. Then, the stained tape serves to separate your surface consciousness from your subconscious.

Let us consider the reason for this with an example of a newborn infant.

Although it may not be apparent to the parents, infants have interactions with the spiritual realm up until about the age of two, or between two and three years of age. You might occasionally observe a baby looking in a random direction, smiling and laughing, or waving happily. This is because its own guardian spirit from the other world is present, and is encouraging the baby. In return, it is responding with joy.

In this way, the mind of a newborn baby is originally innocent, and it is able to communicate with the spirits of the heavenly realm, or the other world. However, as the baby grows, its mind gets cloudier and cloudier as it acquires more selfish wants.

The infant might want to have something in a certain way or be the center of the parents' attention or want more milk, food, or a certain toy. When it does not get all it wants or things do not go as it wishes, the infant becomes more and more selfish.

When such selfish thoughts develop, the infant's mind becomes clouded, and eventually becomes separated from the spirits in the heavenly realm, evolving into a very worldly being.

In this way, we could say that the difference between the existence of the other world and the existence of this world is based on selfish desires. Selfish desire, or egotism, is the act of putting oneself or one's needs first. It is as though a curtain has been drawn on a window to prevent one from peering through.

The effect would be that the curtain blocks one from communicating with the spiritual world. If that is the case, if the curtain were opened one would be able to perceive the outside world. This is what you can expect to happen.

We could then consider what it would take to open the curtain. The curtain, in this case, corresponds to the cloudy part of the thought tape.

I have just explained how the clouding of the mind develops, giving the example of an infant. Later, as the infant grows into a child and starts school, more issues will develop.

In many instances, problems will emerge from comparing one's own circumstances with those of others. One might have thoughts such as, "That girl has a better dress than me," or "The boy sitting next to me always brings a more delicious lunch from home," or "The girl next to me does better schoolwork than me," or "The boy sitting in front of me in class runs faster than I can," or "The student in the first row is always praised by the teacher." In this way, comparing oneself to others will work to draw close the curtains of ego of the child's mind.

The curtains are actually sheer, but as one adds more layers of them, they combine to become less transparent to light.

As the child progresses to upper elementary school, there may be an awakening to the opposite sex. There is no worry when admiration of the opposite sex is pure, but it may become something other than that.

At the junior high school level, children tend to become preoccupied with sex. This can be expressed as "worldly delusion," which is hard to rid from one's mind. When a teenager tries to concentrate on some subject to study, thoughts of the opposite sex keep returning to his or her mind.

These feelings become even stronger in senior high school.

Additionally, during the high school years students will start to develop an interest in society. This is a time of great anxiety for teenagers as they try to determine what they want to be. What should be done after graduation? Is college the answer? Should one find a job right away? This is the time when a decision has to be made. Thus, they start to face issues that will eventually affect their standing in society.

Those aiming for higher education have to take university entrance exams, and quite a few of them experience the setback of failing the exam at the age of eighteen or nineteen. At times like this, it can cause their minds to become clouded.

On the other hand, others who successfully passed their exams may develop feelings of conceit. It is feeling that they are better and special, and this would also cause their minds to become clouded.

In their college years, egoistic thoughts may emerge as students interact with society, causing them to be attracted to confrontation and destruction. Instead of studying seriously, some may get involved in radical social activities and live rebelliously. Then some do not concentrate on studying but just float through college. On the other hand, there are others who are driven to study hard and become overly focused in a limited field of work.

Then, the students seek jobs and enter the workplace.

Once they start working, they experience issues with their superiors, subordinates, peers, and the opposite sex, again causing clouds to develop and cover their minds.

They may also experience the situation of marriage. If they cannot find their ideal mates, they will suffer; on the other hand, even if they do marry their ideal partner, they may face the gap between what is ideal and reality, and they suffer. When they have children, their living costs increase and they experience problems just to maintain their livelihood.

Workplace issues such as transfers and overseas assignments may await. There are also problems with getting along with co-workers, career advancement, or demotion.

People experience challenges such as these.

At home, there are matters of dealing with illness or relationships with parents and siblings in adult life. In addition, as their children grow older, the parents will start to have problems with their children's schooling in the same manner they used to experience. Also, as the children mature, the parents will encounter issues with the marriage of their children.

Reaching mid-life, people in their forties and fifties start to worry about their life after retirement. They start to question themselves as to what kind of lives they will have after their working career. They will ask things like: "Will I be entitled to retirement benefits?" "What will happen to my pension?" or "Will I be able to repay my debts?"

In their old age, people may not get along with their children or in-laws, as reflected in the comment, "I love my grandchildren but my son's wife doesn't listen to me." There are many problems of this sort.

If we view our lives in this way, we will experience many worrying concerns, although this way of looking at our lives is a negative approach. Incurring life's problems, we gradually develop clouds that cast shadows over our minds.

It would be good if we could clear out the clouds one by one, as soon as they appear. However, the clouds will gradually accumulate, and our minds become increasingly stained with dark colors. Then, we will not be able to attune ourselves to the heavenly realm, unable to see through all the stains on our thought tape.

3

Reflective Meditation

I have mentioned the clouds that cover the thought tape, and actually, there are ways to remove them. The methods were once taught by Shakyamuni Buddha in ancient India.

He advocated the teachings called the Eightfold Path. He practiced daily meditation, reflecting on what he thought and did during the day, measuring them against "seeing rightly," "thinking rightly," "speaking rightly," and so on. He taught this method to his disciples. Shakyamuni viewed life as similar to keeping a tally of daily bookkeeping; each day we have to close our accounts and examine our actions and what was in our minds. He himself practiced this idea every day. Thus, reflective meditation was the most important in daily practices.

The main concerns that he concentrated on in his self-reflection were "Did I experience any disturbance in my mind? Did I get irritated? Did I get angry? Did I become conceited? Did I bear any grudges? Did I feel any jealousy?" He measured his mind with such yardsticks.

Right View – seeing rightly

As part of his methodology, Shakyamuni taught the perspective of reflecting on whether one saw rightly.

Right View or seeing rightly can be difficult for a human being. It is not easy for one to measure another rightly. Looking at another person's existence rightly can be a great challenge. In the matter of looking at a person, there would be many different kinds of evaluations. The fact that there are such a variety of evaluations means, in the truest sense of the word, that we could not see the person rightly.

Regarding "not seeing rightly," the same issue applies when looking at ourselves. Usually, we cannot see ourselves as we are seen from the eyes of others. Also, we could say that we cannot see ourselves as we are seen from the eyes of God or Buddha, and it would be the painful truth.

In this way, even the simple act of "seeing" is quite a challenge. It would be extremely difficult to try to observe accurately from the perspective of the mind of God or Buddha.

Right Thought – thinking rightly

The next teaching is Right Thought, which means thinking rightly. It is difficult to know whether you are thinking rightly.

Reflect on how you have been during the day: What kinds of thoughts deserve to be considered right thoughts? Did you have any bad thoughts about anyone? Have you been true to yourself? Did you deceive anyone? Did you give in to any earthly desires? Examine yourself on these points. Examine thoroughly the thoughts that passed through your mind. Examine your thoughts, not just the words you spoke out loud. This is a necessary step.

Right Speech – speaking rightly

Next comes Right Speech, which means speaking rightly. Reflection of Right Speech is also a very important task for building utopia on earth.

There is a theory that all misery in the world derives from words – words that express hatred or anger, words that ridicule or torment others, words of worry or complaint – they ultimately create sorrow and suffering in our lives.

Therefore, it could be said that modifying the use of our words provides us with one of the keys to happiness.

Complaining will cause clouds to cover over your mind, but it would be hard to be aware of unless someone else pointed it out to you. What causes complaining is, after all, your sense of dissatisfaction over the gap between what you want and reality. This is where the discontent arises.

The same could be said about anger. Anger occurs when hatred rises up from your heart. When hatred swells up, it causes anger, which is then vented onto someone else.

There are also words that express jealousy or suspicion. There would be no problem if one just kept silent. If such words were not uttered and instead remained in one's mind, the poison would not come out. But if let out, the poison infects others, giving rise to contagion.

Therefore, it is very important to choose the right words when you speak. When you look back on your activities during the day and find that you were not successful in saying the right words, you must reflect on it and make sure to speak the right words the following day.

Right Action – working rightly

Self-reflection of Right Action involves questioning whether you have worked in the right way. When you look back on your day, you can examine whether you have done your job rightly. If you are a company employee, you should ask yourself, "Did I do a job that really contributed to the company, or did I do the job in a half-hearted manner? Did I pay full attention to my job?"

If you are a housewife, check if you have lived your life to the fullest, being grateful that you have been given the opportunity to refine your soul as you take care of your family and home.

You should reflect on your roles as a housewife: Did I care for my children properly? Did I properly do my job? What did I do for my husband? Have I thought of things to help my family do better? Have I saved enough money, and not spent any of it on wasteful things? Was any time misused in the education of my children? Is everything going well in the household? Have I made sure that my husband will be able to go to work tomorrow in a good mood?

These are points for housewives to reflect on.

There is also the kind of reflection of whether you are satisfying what is expected of you according to your standing. When you were newly hired at your job, there was a particular set of requirements you had to satisfy. As you are promoted up the ladder to become a section chief and have subordinates, the job requirements of a chief are definitely more than those of a new recruit. A different mindset is necessary for the higher position. When you advance to department head or become a board member, you will have more and more authority and responsibilities.

People naturally expect to be promoted, but there are reasons for being promoted, and the higher your position, the more responsibilities you must assume. Are you fulfilling your responsibilities?

When you are a company president, you cannot make judgments and decisions based solely on your own personal circumstances, because the destiny and happiness of all the company employees will be affected. When a president makes a decision, it may often be a crucial one and made after serious consideration, done with prayers to heaven. Would subordinates know what it takes to make executive decisions? It is a matter that deserves consideration.

Right Living – living a rightful life

There is also Right Living. This means to live in the right way. You are expected to examine whether you lead a regular life, a life that you are not ashamed of as a child of God or a child of Buddha.

Right Effort – making right efforts to keep on the path

With Right Effort, you would check to see if you are striving to keep on the path of Truth. Have you studied Buddha's Truth and done something to advance on the path of Truth? What have you done for the happiness of others? Have you ever prayed for others? Did you have a sense of gratitude for God or Buddha? You are expected to reflect on your efforts on these points.

Right Will – using your willpower in the right way

There is also Right Will. This means using your willpower or concentrated thoughts in the right way. This path is related to prayers, a practice that is available for all people.

The thought waves of various people are being dispersed around the globe, and if these waves are negative, they will cause conditions in the world to become chaotic.

Therefore, each of our thoughts must be of a beneficial nature; they should be positive, constructive, and cheerful. In this sense, being in control of your willpower is extremely important. You need to emit the right thought waves.

Right Meditation – practice meditation in the right way

The last teaching in the Eightfold Path is Right Meditation, or practicing meditation in the right way. It is important to have time to concentrate your thoughts inward to ensure that you might communicate with God or Buddha, or your guardian and guiding spirits as you reflect on the day or the past.

In total, such practice constitutes what is called reflective meditation.

This type of meditation may not necessarily be of a constructive nature or help to bring progress. But it will at least be a way to eliminate the realm of hell in this world on earth and in the other world.

If people become well-practiced in this kind of reflective meditation, they can at the very least avoid going to hell. And those who are residing in hell would be able to get out of it. Also, we would be able to eliminate the hellish world on earth. It is a practice that wields great and formidable power.

Therefore, reflective meditation must be brought back in general practice. It is important to revive this reflective meditation of Shakyamuni Buddha's time.

Besides, this practice was not only taught by Shakyamuni Buddha. Christianity has had the practice of confession. The essence of doing penance before God to apologize for your sins is very similar to reflective meditation in Buddhism.

Japanese Shintoism practices ritual purification and exorcism, done by standing before gods with a purified mind and heart, or sitting humbly before them. Basically, it is also similar to reflective meditation.

In the historical time of Moses, importance was placed on vows made to God. The meaning of "testament" in the Old and New Testaments of the Bible is "covenant," or "a promise between God and mankind." They are reminders to live up to our promises to God to observe His commandments and serve as the basis of self-reflection.

Did I break any promise to God today? Did I break the commandment, "Thou shalt not kill?" Did I break the commandment, "Thou shalt not covet thy neighbor's wife?" Did I break the commandment, "Thou shalt not bear false witness against thy neighbor?" Did I betray God? Have I lived up to God's expectations?

Every day, people were expected to reflect on whether they had honored their contract with God. They practiced self-reflection in this way.

Similar practices can be found in all the religions I have mentioned above. Everything, in the end, leads to an attitude of pursuing and exploring the right way of living as a child of God, a child of Buddha. I would like you to consider reflective meditation from this perspective.

4

Opening the Spiritual Pathway

After becoming well-practiced in reflective meditation, you may experience the phenomenon of having a spiritual pathway opened to you. This phenomenon can be explained as follows: When you draw open the layers of curtains that cover your mind one by one, as if cleaning away a fog shrouding your mind, at some point, the light will begin to shine in from somewhere, or you will gradually begin to see the outside. Imagine with this example how the phenomenon of opening a spiritual pathway occurs.

When your spiritual pathway is opened, you will first become able to communicate with your guardian spirit either directly or indirectly. When you meditate, you may hear the voice of your guardian spirit as if it comes from within your heart.

It is also possible for a guardian spirit to speak using one's voice to give spiritual messages. Depending on the person, a guardian spirit may provide a variety of inspirational messages using the person's hands. This is called "automatic writing."

At times the communications are not just typical conversations but various kinds of revelations and inspirational thoughts.

These are what can occur in the phenomena of opening spiritual pathways for different individuals.

In opening your spiritual pathway, the first step would be to communicate with your guardian spirit. It is possible for anyone to communicate with his or her own guardian spirit in some way to the extent effort was made, regardless of one's latent or inborn ability. If you regularly practice reflective meditation, firmly comprehend Buddha's Truth, and put your studies into practice, you will find that your spiritual pathway will gradually open up.

There are different forms of the phenomenon of opening a spiritual pathway. The various channels that can be taken include such forms as indirect inspiration, direct inspiration, spiritual speech, automatic writing, spiritual hearing or clairaudience, and spiritual sight or clairvoyance. In some manner, you will be able to experience the situation of being able to hear the opinion of your guardian spirit. This is possible for everyone.

However, it is generally understood that your guardian spirit must first allow you permission to open a spiritual pathway. It is normal for a guardian spirit to allow a spiritual pathway to open when it feels that it is good for the person, according to a certain set of prerequisite criteria. When the guardian spirit is not sure whether it would be beneficial to open, the matter would then be taken up by higher-level divine spirits to allow permission. This is how the matter would be handled.

Moreover, it is also possible to open a spiritual pathway when aided by the light of a greatly gifted psychic who is a great guiding spirit of light, when such a spirit is incarnated on earth. However, in this case, great caution is required after one's spiritual pathway is opened. If the person is not aware of the risk involved, evil spirits can enter through the open channel and confuse the person's mind. Such a danger is involved.

Opening a spiritual pathway is itself a very natural and conceivably sound act, but it is very difficult to maintain one's state of mind afterward. For this reason, having the mystical power of *rojin* is critically important, as I will explain later in this book. It is vital to examine yourself to see if you can live a respectable life in this world even after your spiritual pathway has been opened.

You must be very careful not to be overjoyed simply because your spiritual pathway is opened or you can hear the voices of spirits, as can be seen in various groups of spiritual seekers.

There are many different kinds of spiritual dialogues. In fact, it is very rare to interact with higher spirits. Instead, the most commonly heard voices are those of earthbound spirits, lower-level spirits, or animal spirits, all of which try to tempt you in some way or another.

In order to protect yourself from these kinds of temptations, it is important to live humbly every day, try hard to rid yourself of egoistic desires, greed, or conceit, and free yourself of frustration, anger, envy, complaining, or jealousy.

It is vital to keep your mind transparent. Living with a clear and transparent state of mind is the secret to preventing your mind from attracting low-grade spiritual influence.

I would like you to be especially careful about what I have mentioned here.

5

The First Step toward Enlightenment

There are many people who regard "opening their spiritual pathway" as being equal to enlightenment.

The response to that idea is that, truthfully, we could think of it as the first step toward enlightenment. There is great significance in opening a spiritual pathway as one goes about living one's daily life, as it would provide more opportunity to awaken to Buddha's Truth, to a spiritual view of life.

No matter what kind of life a person lives as a result of opening a spiritual pathway, that person will be able to say, "I had a glimpse of the spiritual world or the world of gods and Buddha while I was still humanly alive." In this context, it can be regarded as an advancement, or progress for the soul. Therefore, it can be referred to as the first step toward enlightenment.

However, it is a mistake to take this spiritual phenomenon, the opening of the spiritual pathway, to be equal to enlightenment. You need to understand that this is only the first step, which may act like a catalyst that leads you to enlightenment.

If you misunderstand the phenomenon of "opening a spiritual pathway" to be exactly the same as attaining enlightenment, the result will be devastating. If you listen to the voice of whatever spirit and accept all that is said to be truth, you will be dominated by it.

Such a spirit will take total control of you. If you become conceited, thinking you are enlightened, you will then be manipulated by the voice of such a spirit and be led in the wrong direction.

Therefore, after opening your spiritual pathway, one of the most important things to do is verify, even when listening to the words of high spirits, or your guardian and guiding spirits. You have to filter them through the teachings of the Eightfold Path. This attitude is important.

It may be possible that you are hearing random spiritual voices because there is something within you that is strongly attracted to them. This could happen.

Even if what you hear seems to be the voice of a high-level spirit, it is necessary to re-examine it through the filter of the Eightfold Path. If you are not totally convinced, take time to consider the message again to see if it is right or not, that you are comfortable with it. This is an important attitude to take.

However, you should not be overly skeptical. Although a high spirit may send you a true revelation, if you feel you have the right to evaluate it from your own earthly viewpoint, the revelation would mean nothing. It would be as if there is no God or Buddha, but only you who matters.

Such a person would just be self-centered and egoistic. For this type of person, having spiritual abilities or being able to hear revelations would be meaningless. You must not be like the kind of person who is conceited and who puts themself first.

However, even if the voice is considered to be that of a high spirit, it is important to apply the filter to check whether heeding the voice would pave the way for your improvement. This is the first point to be aware of.

The second point is to examine whether it is a path that would lead to the harm of others. You must make sure you will not cause harm to others.

The third point would be to make an overall judgment whether what the voices imply would conform to the mind of God or Buddha.

Truly, it would be very difficult to satisfy all these points.

For example, suppose you are in the middle of a job search and receive a revelation from a high spirit recommending you to get a job at a certain company.

As you reflect on your situation, you are not quite sure you want to take the suggested job. You will have some doubt, but you feel you will not know for sure until you get the job. Then on further thought, you feel that the job is not too bad, and you may be rather comfortable with it. Thus, the first point is satisfied.

Then, you can examine the job with the next criterion, whether or not taking this job would cause harm to others. If you are convinced that it is not harmful to others, then the second condition would be met.

The third checkpoint is to examine whether it suits the mind of God or Buddha. After considering the third condition, you feel that taking the job will help you better contribute to the creation of a utopia on earth.

You might think, "This job reasonably satisfies all three criteria, if not perfectly." You then decide to take the position and leave all consequences to heaven. You will be sure of your decision made through the above process.

However, if you take another track in the same situation by relying on your own views, thinking, "No matter if it was a high spirit, gods, or Buddha who gave me the revelation, I will do what I think is right. I will definitely find the job that I think is right; there is no need to consider any other option if I don't feel like it," then in this way, you would simply be following your egoistic desires.

While it is necessary to examine the revelation or inspiration you received according to each of the reasonable criteria, in the end, it is also important to free yourself of earthly attachment and listen to the heavenly voice with a detached attitude.

At this point, the most important element is the sense of trust. It is to leave everything to heaven, giving full trust. In other words, it is important to believe, "If God or Buddha is watching over me, there will be no unfortunate outcome."

This does not mean to mindlessly follow heavenly power but to leave the final decision to God or Buddha. Then, if you think you can choose a life that would serve God or Buddha in any way, evil spirits would not be able to interfere with your life.

If one lives with the belief that "All I want to do is make a profit. I will be happy only if I can satisfy my own desires," one will encounter many problems. On the contrary, if one has the attitude of "Ultimately, I want to be useful to God and Buddha," demons will not find a way to interfere or intrude on your life. This is the truth about the spiritual world.

Therefore, those who have taken the first step toward enlightenment, having opened a spiritual pathway, must make sure to live humbly and carefully. And they need to constantly check to see that their lives are aligned as servants of God or Buddha, as a part of them, as volunteers.

If they could see themselves as volunteers in the service of God or Buddha, without expecting anything in return, then all that is left would be to remain true to that belief.

In any case, opening a spiritual pathway is indeed the first step toward enlightenment, but do not let it make you proud. You must not become conceited; you have to know that it is only a beginning and there is much, much more to expect.

In the second step of opening your spiritual pathway, you will be able to communicate not only with your own guardian spirit but also with higher-leveled divine spirits and guiding spirits.

Moreover, it is commonly said that when communicating with such high-level divine spirits, the stature of both speakers must be equal.

For example, in order to receive a spiritual message from Nichiren Shonin [the Japanese Buddhist high priest of the thirteenth century], you need to be of the same caliber as he is. Your character should be as accomplished as his, as virtuous as his. Your level of intelligence, sensitivity, and enlightenment should be the same as his.

As you see, you must have a capacity of such magnitude to be able to communicate with a high-level divine spirit.

There are many instances of people claiming that they can communicate with certain well-known spirits. This occurs in many places, but you must recognize that the people who receive spiritual guidance and those spirits sending them are on the same level.

Therefore, we need to pay attention to the behavior and achievement of those receivers who are still living on earth. You must know that one cannot receive a message from a high spirit unless one has an equivalent level of stature.

In other words, you must realize that high-level guiding spirits will not just come down to any random person to give guidance. The guidance will only be given to someone who is regarded to be accomplished, dynamic, and as capable as the high spirits.

Of course, there are difficulties in making judgments of this sort because there are people all around who claim to have such qualities and abilities. Therefore, it would be necessary to examine the caliber of these people objectively to determine if they really possess positive aspects to convince people in society.

Fear and apprehension can be involved in the experience of opening your spiritual pathway, but when you overcome them, it can bring you even greater joy and a broader perspective of life.

It is a path full of possibility, so please do not be afraid and live courageously.

If you have your spiritual pathway opened, as long as you have the attitude to make humble efforts every day, you will not have to worry about experiencing a downfall. I hope that you will have the courage to proceed on this path. This is my sincere prayer for you.

Chapter 3

Different Kinds of
Spiritual Ability

1

Spiritual Sight

In this chapter, I will discuss various kinds of spiritual abilities.

First, I want to introduce one of the most representative of these: spiritual sight.

Most of you may know that spiritual sight is the ability to see things that are not of this world.

Specifically, it is the ability to see spirits or figures of spirits or to peer into the other world. In some cases, it involves the ability to have a vivid vision of scenes from the future, and in other cases scenes from the past.

In these situations, it is the ability to see things that cannot usually be seen with our eyes in normal circumstances. It could be called psychic seeing.

There are quite a lot of people in the world who claim to be psychic visionaries, but in reality, psychic vision is only what a particular person can see. No one else can share the same experience, so it would be impossible to verify or relive it. Therefore, people who associate with the self-claimed psychic are put in the position of either believing or not believing that he or she can really see spirits.

There are some people who are not necessarily thought of as mentally disturbed just because they see psychic visions; they may actually be exercising their spiritual abilities. But others may be seen as insane even though they utilize the same ability. In fact, some people who are hospitalized in mental hospitals often see and hear things that normal people cannot see or hear.

In that sense, it cannot be denied that there is a dangerous aspect to this ability.

Then, how is spiritual sight possible? Let me explain this point further.

Human eyes, as you know, have lenses. The retina receives images of light that are reflected from this physical world, but things beyond the limits of this world would not be seen. Therefore, what is seen by spiritual sight is not what can be seen by the physical eye. Objects of spiritual sight are seen by what is called the spiritual eye. It is the spiritual eyes that see things that are of a spiritual nature.

If you ask where the spiritual eye is located, you can basically think of it as in the same area as the physical human eyes. As the eye chakra is said to be located between the eyebrows in esoteric Buddhism and yoga, the nerve center of the eyes is located mainly in the area between the eyebrows. It is an energy center and is used to see various forms of spirits.

It is a very strange sensation, but this secret cannot be unlocked without understanding the relevance between spirit and body.

It is commonly known that the eyes register the outside light as it is reflected on one's retina, and then signals are sent to the brain for comprehension; this is the way one recognizes what one sees, just as one's eardrums receive outside vibrations to be transmitted to one's brain to be recognized as sounds. However, in reality, the brain itself does not perceive, but is the organ that receives and organizes information from external sources.

If so, then there must be some entity that further analyzes, perceives, and understands the information that has been transmitted to and organized by the brain. This entity would be the mind. It is the mind, the center of the soul, that evaluates the information. Therefore, it can be said that spiritual sight is actually seeing things with the mind's eye.

In considering what can trigger one to acquire spiritual sight, I believe ultimately that this spiritual ability is based on spiritual sensitivity.

However, regardless of your spiritual sensitivity, it may be possible to see spiritual images. For example, you may see a ghost in a graveyard, or you may suddenly have to deal with the death of a family member and see their spiritual body. In such cases, the energy of the deceased person's thoughts is so intense to the extent that their image often materializes, appearing before you in a physically visible form.

Usually, spiritual sight itself is not accidental; in many cases, if you want to see it, you would be able to do so.

Spiritual sight can start with being able to perceive the aura of a living person. If you look around the head of the person, you would see a pale light, a glow radiating out of it. Possibly, when encountering an angel of light incarnated on earth, you might be able to see their entire body emanating a golden light. Oppositely, you might vaguely recognize when a person is possessed by a negative spirit. This is the first stage.

In the second stage of having spiritual sight, you would be able to see spiritual forms more clearly. At this stage, not only would you be able to see a person's aura, but also their guardian spirit, and in the case of the possessed, the entity that is possessing the person.

At the third stage of spiritual sight, you would be able to see not only the forms but also be able to recognize the essence of any spirit: "What is the nature of the spirit? What does it think? What is its intention?" Upon encountering the spirit, you would be able to distinguish these points in clear detail. This is the ability called *kanjizai* that can be exercised at this stage.

With this ability, as soon as you meet someone you will instantly comprehend their entire being, immediately being able to determine the identity of the spirit and its intentions. Having reached this point, your spiritual sight is almost complete.

The most common style of exercising spiritual sight or clairvoyance is to focus thoughts on the spiritual images, with the eyes closed. But some people are capable of spiritual sight with their eyes open. In such cases, to avoid confusion with their regular vision, the spiritual images would be viewed as if on a small monochrome screen in front of one's forehead, centered between the eyebrows.

This is the first of the spiritual abilities, spiritual sight.

2

Spiritual Hearing

An ability that is often mentioned together with spiritual sight is the ability of spiritual hearing, or clairaudience. It is the ability to hear the voices of spirits.

This ability can be described as having an auditory experience when no one else is near. It would be similar to hearing sounds like whispering or a person's voice, as if someone were speaking into your ear while you sleep.

These seemingly auditory disorders may include ringing sensations in your ear or hearing voices of various people. In psychiatry, it is called auditory hallucination, but more commonly these might be evidence of negative forms of spiritual hearing that occur as the result of spiritual disturbances. If you are afflicted by an evil spirit and it persists in bothering you daily, you may be hearing the whispering of such a spirit. You might call it spiritual disturbance, but in fact, it is just another type of spiritual hearing.

However, being able to hear the voice of an evil spirit that is present does not mean it is an instance of spiritual hearing in the true sense. Spiritual abilities must align with Buddha's Truth. The ability attained by a person who lives rightly is not the same as hearing the muttering of any random spirit.

In other words, there can be two types of spiritual hearing.

The spiritual hearing of external sounds, or voices coming from outside of you, is primarily caused by spiritual disturbances and is often the whispering of evil or low-grade spirits. It is like whispering into one's ear.

If it is real spiritual hearing, it would not sound like whispering; rather, the words come from deep within your chest. Real spiritual hearing is when you can hear a message resonating from within your chest, from inside your body. In this way, such words express truthfulness and sincerity.

There is also another way to receive messages that is somewhat different from spiritual hearing: Some people receive messages in the form of inspiration. It is a way of acquiring specific images that appear in the mind instantaneously.

In some cases, inspiration can come in the form of certain ideas or images that appear in your mind as if being displayed on a TV screen.

There are two kinds of spiritual hearing. One is when messages are received as revelations from heaven, and the other is when they are received as voices from deep within, voices emanating from within your heart. In these cases, the messages are most often considered genuine.

On the other hand, if you are persistently disturbed by some kind of presence, and experience the spiritual hearing of voices coming from outside your body, it is likely to be something different, and you will need to be very vigilant.

So when is true spiritual hearing ability experienced?

After all, people who are psychic mediums can achieve a state where they are usually capable of psychic hearing. This means that a chasm already exists between their surface consciousness and subconscious. Therefore, they can communicate with their own guardian and guiding spirits, but if their state of mind is tended in the wrong direction, they would be susceptible to temptation by evil spirits.

In reality, quite a few people have the ability of spiritual hearing, but at most, only 2% to 3% of them can really hear the voices of spirits from heaven. The remaining 97% to 98% are possessed by low-level spirits, animal spirits, or evil spirits, and would be influenced by their suggestions. That is the characteristic of the majority of psychics.

Because of this, seekers of spiritual truth must be very vigilant. You have to be very careful. This is how I feel.

3

Spiritual Speech

The next ability, that of spiritual speech, can in a broad sense be included with the ability of spiritual hearing.

I have previously published a good number of spiritual messages with various content. [As of July 2021 more than 600 books have been published of interviews with spirits recorded in view of live audiences.] These interviews provide examples of spiritual speech. Spiritual speech is the situation in which spirits are allowed to speak using the voice of a particular person.

Letting a spirit speak utilizing someone's voice has been a typical form of spiritual ability since ancient times. It has been practiced for millennia. In ancient times, it was identified with shamanic ability. There are accounts of certain priestesses, oracles, and spell-casters who had these abilities.

There is also a considerable level of difference in what is said by people with this spiritual ability.

Examples of low-level spiritual speech are those messages from the various spirits that take over a psychic's voice and speak through them. In many cases, they are a variety of animal spirits that are being given voice.

There are also mediums who invite the spirits of the dead to speak through them. They do this for people inquiring about deceased family members, such as parents or grandparents, in order to deliver messages.

However, this type of psychic ability merely shows susceptibility to influences from spirits that are usually not high spirits. Those who channel messages from spirits think of themselves as messengers of gods, but in reality, they often are not. When claiming they can call upon the spirits of the dead, it is usually an ability to call upon the departed who have fallen into hell. Those in hell all crave for some release so that they can express themselves; they may approach such mediums to get their messages channeled.

This is possible because even if you are not able to communicate with high spirits, your thoughts can instantly be broadcast to many different realms, as the mind is said to have the ability to attune to three thousand worlds.

However, attuning to higher spiritual levels, or to high spirits, would be extremely difficult. In order to receive a spiritual message from a high-level spirit, you need to have practiced a certain amount of spiritual discipline.

Now, I need to explain the mechanism of communicating with the Spirit World. Many people may wonder and want to know how communication with the Spirit World is done; they want to know how the process actually works.

The realm comprising spiritual vibrations really exists. There are reports describing the spiritual world as if seen by physical eyes, explaining how mountains, valleys, and oceans would look, or how people are, but they are only versions of how things look through human senses.

In reality, such descriptions do not represent the true spiritual states, but are merely attempts at interpretation; the other world consists of spiritual vibrations. These vibrations occur on many different wavelengths that are sent out.

They are just like TV signals. Electromagnetic waves fly about in the invisible realm, and they are received and visualized in various ways.

Therefore, in order to communicate with the spiritual world, people on earth cannot communicate unless they emit the same wavelengths as those of the spiritual world.

Channel reception for television or radio must match the frequency of the broadcast signal; otherwise, you would not be able to receive any broadcasts. Spiritual communication would be exactly the same circumstance. It is essential for a person to meet the strict conditions in order to be on the same frequency to receive the spiritual messages of the high spirits.

In this world, there are often people who claim to embody well-known high-level spirits or gods. Also, there are many people who say they can hear the voices of high spirits that are present in shrines and temples, religious sites, or other places. It is a very difficult task to identify what might be a precious stone in a pile of rocks, so to speak. In the end, it comes down to the character of the person.

The key measure is to check whether the person making the claim has the same character as the high spirit.

However, in regard to character, it is not easy for an ordinary person to measure the level of someone's moral values. So I would like to suggest some criteria on which to judge whether a message was really sent from a high spirit or whether the person claiming to receive a message truly fits the role.

First of all, there are special conditions that should be met before a high spirit would deliver spiritual messages and for making certain that the person is qualified to receive such messages.

The first condition is that the receiver's mind should always be in harmony. If one is easily angered or becomes upset when faced with criticism, one would not be qualified. Also, if there is an extreme tendency in one's mind, such as a very strong feeling of hatred or jealousy, being antagonistic, or having an abnormal sense of pride or self-deprecation, it is sure that one would never attune to high spirits.

Harmony of one's mind is essential, as this was what Shakyamuni Buddha taught again and again more than 2,500 years ago:

A tathagata is one who has achieved emancipation. An emancipated person is at peace, not attached to anything. For such a person, every day is lived as if a river flows peacefully and smoothly. This is the state of mind of a tathagata.

This is what he taught repeatedly, and it is possible to find the record of this teaching in the Buddhist scriptures.

Harmony of mind, in other words, means whether you are living peacefully every day without any disturbances in your mind.

People who are possessed by evil spirits or demons are usually quick to become enraged. It is not an exaggeration to say that if one tends to become easily angered, irritated, or unsatisfied, one would not have the stature to be attuned to high spirits.

Religions are practiced by many people in many places throughout the world, and because religious believers have teachers that they follow, there should be observance of the lives of those who are called teachers.

You might encounter a person who proclaims there will be a punishment from the gods and curses brought on you for things that have been done, or who makes threats, saying, "If you leave the group, you will die," or "You will be cursed if you don't join this group." Perhaps this person would say to another, "You are cursed by an ancestor from a past generation in your family ancestry, and if you want to be saved, you have to have a certain ceremony ministered," and then asks for an exorbitant amount of money to perform the ceremony.

These kinds of people are usually religious leaders who have been completely captivated by evil spirits. It is wisest to stay away from such people.

Therefore, harmony of the mind is the first priority.

The second condition to receive spiritual messages is by measuring one's record of achievement. This is what I have taught over and over again in Happy Science: "If you really are a person of great stature, you should be able to show a purposeful number of relevant achievements."

Being an angel of light, one would certainly need to achieve what is expected of an angel. In the same manner, it is necessary to examine if a religious leader is really helping people to improve themselves, to guide them in the right direction, and to see if the people who have received guidance have gotten better. This kind of attitude is important. Important questions for self-reflection would be, "Have I truly made people happy? Have I made a difference in their lives?"

The first measure is to determine whether the people the leader interacted with have become happy, have improved their lives, to see if they have gotten better as human beings.

There is also the question of "what kind of behavior do the leaders really show?" While they talk of saving people, what about their actual deeds, and whether they are doing what they say must be done? They may only be doing things to protect their own groups and constantly slander or defame others. If that is how they behave, you cannot be sure that these kinds of people deserve to be called angels of light.

Therefore, their records of achievement are important. These achievements would include the sum total of their actions – what they have done, said, or written. They would be judged based on such achievements.

If someone claims, "I am a Great Guiding Spirit of Light," then they should be asked what they have done to deserve that claim. All of the historically known guiding spirits of light have left many good works behind. There is reliable proof to show what they have done.

Usually, if a person has not gained worldly recognition by the age of sixty or seventy, then the person cannot be considered a great figure. As the saying goes, "If a man reaches the age of forty or fifty and has still not become known, then he is no one to be in awe of"

[Analects of Confucius]. During some point in life, a person of great stature will inevitably demonstrate outstanding quality showing the radiance of their soul. The innate greatness of their soul will be exercised.

Therefore, it is important to carefully examine what has already been accomplished by any person who claims to be a great figure or a great angel. If the person lived a very difficult life, a life filled with feelings of inferiority, but successfully overcame such adversity, it would be an accomplishment to be respected. On the contrary, if the person boasts of being a great figure as a way to compensate for an inferiority complex, then it might be concluded that their life story is suspicious.

No matter what kind of hardship a person experiences, a truly great person will be able to show the radiance of their soul. So you should look very carefully to see if there is any sign of such radiance.

The third criterion to consider when a person claims to be conveying a message from a high spirit is the actual content of the message.

Many spiritual messages are falsely attributed using the names of the high spirits. However, it is very difficult for people living on earth to determine whether the claiming person is giving the true name. It would be almost impossible to verify the words of those who lived 800, 1,200, or 2,000 years ago. Finding answers to questions about those times would be difficult because of the scarcity of materials left from the distant past. So the criterion to be evaluated would be the actual content of the spiritual message.

How can we evaluate the content of a spiritual message from a high spirit? There are three aspects to determine if it is genuine when evaluating the content.

The first aspect is the sense of nobility reflected in the spiritual message. If the words were spoken by a former great person on earth, did they show a certain elegance? Did they display a certain nobility of character? Was there some kind of eminence, or did they have a profound nature?

The point is whether a certain dignity is shown. If it were genuinely a high spirit, the message would not be just a boast or to criticize people. The words of a high spirit naturally give out a certain nobility and grace. This is a very important point to consider.

I believe that this grace includes an attitude of humility. The greater the person, the humbler the attitude they may take. A true high spirit rarely comments on their own greatness. There might be times when there is a particular need for it to be affirmed, but at most times a high spirit behaves humbly. In this way, you can examine if there is an attitude of humility.

The second aspect in judging the content of a spiritual message is whether the content points in a direction that would lead people to happiness. You need to examine whether the content and purpose of the spiritual message would give support for the happiness of people. You should be wary if the message content is filled with phrases that would cause people misery. If the content includes guidance to do things that would cause people misery, it would be a serious problem. It would be wise to avoid heeding such messages.

This second aspect is to judge whether there is an enthusiastic effort to bring happiness or provide even the slightest improvement to people.

If the spiritual messages are centered on negative contents, like "You will be cursed," or "All your family will die because of such and such omens," there should be cause for suspicion. It is unthinkable that a high spirit would say such things except in extreme circumstances. Generally, messages that are full of threats, cajolery, and intimidation, which only make people feel insecure when hearing the dark predictions, are to be questioned.

The essential point in judging a message's credibility is to see if there are words of hope with the express purpose of bringing happiness to people.

The third aspect in judging a spiritual message is to see if it explains the spiritual world clearly. It is key that the spirit can explain the workings of the Spirit World.

If a spirit asserts, "There is no such thing as an afterlife," or "There is no reincarnation," you can be sure that they are the announcements of an evil spirit. There are many religious practitioners and psychics in the world, but if some would start to say things like "People do not experience anything like reincarnation," or "There is nothing after death, no afterlife," it is sure that they are completely possessed by evil spirits.

Typically, their first proclamation would be to deny reincarnation. Or else, they would not be able to explain the different levels of the other world, including the world of angels.

A spirit that only speaks of confusion and struggle is not a genuine high spirit.

Angels are usually versed on many subjects to a reasonably intelligent degree. The question is to see if a spirit can clearly explain things.

Therefore, in order to test the authenticity of a person supposedly channeling a message from a high spirit, you can ask the spirit to explain the Spirit World. If you cannot obtain a reasonable explanation, it is likely to be a spirit from hell. This is because such a spirit's experience is limited to the nether world. If all the spirit has encountered has been the continuous torments of hell, there would be no room for imagining what the Spirit World is generally like. Much less could it explain the realms of bodhisattvas and tathagatas. I would recommend that you investigate the matter of whether the spirit could explain these realms.

These are the ways of examining the content of a spiritual message.

In the future, if you meet with a situation like what has been explained so far, I would recommend you to apply these standards to make your judgment.

4

Spiritual Dreams

I would now like to talk about spiritual dreams, a topic that is often discussed.

Many people do not exhibit any direct spiritual abilities when they are awake but do so while asleep. There are many cases of people having spiritual dreams, notably when meeting and talking with the deceased, foreseeing the future, finding out the causes of things, becoming inspired during sleep, or obtaining solutions to make decisions when at a crossroads in their lives. These kinds of spiritual dreams also comprise one of the spiritual abilities.

When asleep, especially during deep, sound sleep, human souls often slip out of people's bodies. During an eight-hour period of sleep, a person's soul can often travel to the Spirit World for a few of those hours, at least two or three of them. When they do, people can have a glimpse of the spiritual world.

Strange things often happen when in the dream state. They are reflections of what happens in the spiritual world.

For example, you might dream you are flying, or diving deep under the sea, or being chased by someone. Such dreams where you find yourself moving through space are usually spiritual dreams; you are often wandering in the Spirit World.

Also, a dream of meeting and talking with someone who has already passed away is a spiritual dream; it is often an occurrence when the soul leaves the body in a dream.

Some people make use of spiritual dreams by first praying for their wishes before going to bed to receive a sign in a dream. This is possible if you have accomplished some degree of spiritual discipline. Your guardian spirits particularly want to provide you with as many answers as possible.

Therefore, if normal people with no psychic ability want to make contact with the Spirit World safely and reliably, experiencing spiritual phenomena in dreams would be a relatively less risky way to do so.

Then, how should one go about setting up conditions to have a spiritual dream?

First of all, it would be difficult if you have too many concerns in your mind before going to bed. Your state of mind before going to sleep is important. If the vibrations of your mind are very disturbed at that time, you will likely become lost in the realm of hell after your soul slips out of your body. If your vibrations are in constant tune, your soul will ascend to the heavenly realms, where you may receive revelations or guidance in a variety of ways.

In that sense, your state of mind before sleep is an important condition in order to have a spiritual dream, and it is necessary to meditate to center your mind before going to sleep. It would be important to reflect on your day or to practice meditation.

When you fall asleep in this state, your mind is usually directed to the heavenly realm, and you can often speak with your guardian spirit.

Therefore, if you wish to talk to your own guardian spirit, you should make sure to harmonize your mind by looking back on the day in self-reflection. With the prayerful request, "Please, my guardian spirit, give me answers to my concerns and problems," said before going to sleep, you will surely receive replies in your dreams.

It does not necessarily mean that a figure in the form of your guardian spirit will appear to you to give you answers; it may appear, for example, in the form of a former school teacher, a friend, or a deceased parent.

In such a way, you will receive answers to your concerns.

You may have a dream of the future. It is also possible to see how circumstances will turn out or how things will look when a problem is solved.

These methods are possible through training. Therefore, if you practice going to sleep without disturbing the wavelengths of your mind, deliberately training yourself to receive inspiration from your guardian spirit, the guidance you will receive becomes clearer and clearer.

When you are distressed by setbacks in business, your studies, or your personal relationships, it is possible to find a remedy by going to sleep with a peaceful mind to receive guidance from your guardian spirit. This is a spiritual ability that is possible even for ordinary people.

5

Foresight

Next, I would like to talk about foresight.

Spiritual ability and foresight are closely bound together. It is often noted that people who have spiritual abilities can somehow see what will happen in the future. It is also said that spirits know people's destinies beforehand. The issue of spiritual ability and foresight is also quite a difficult one.

Foresight means to be able to predict the future, but as we know, it is not necessarily 100% accurate. In other words, it may turn out to be wrong. However, even if a prediction fails, it does not necessarily mean that it makes no sense. This is probably the most difficult aspect in considering foresight.

So how should we consider it? The following can be said about the ability of foresight, which may not always be correct.

In the Spirit World, there is no constraint of time. It means that there is no such thing as a twenty-four-hour period that is measured by a clock. It is because a twenty-four-hour day is determined by the time it takes for the Earth to rotate. However, the rotation of the Earth is no longer relevant in the spiritual world.

In this sense, the habitants of the Spirit World are living an eternal life, not according to time in this world. Therefore, when they say, "Such will happen in such year and such month," it is difficult for them to be exact. So, although high spirits often have visions of things that will really happen, these visions may not always align with the time of this world.

An important attitude regarding predictions is not to be fixated on the timing. If you receive some kind of future vision, you should just think, "That may happen in the future." It might be better not to expect to be more precise than that.

However, it is also true that some high spirits specialize in foresight. Since their ability is expertise in prediction, it seems that they actually have a high degree of accuracy for the future. Still, there is the question of whether they will communicate such details to people on earth. In other words, they may not always choose to do this. There are certain arrangements concerning the future that are subtly kept secret.

The reason why such arrangements exist is that ultimately, people on earth will be bound by the predictions. For their good, the future is kept secret to avoid putting limits on them.

This is an overview of foresight, but basically, this ability is indeed also a means to prove the existence of the spiritual world.

It is difficult for people living in this world to know what will happen in the future, but spirits from the other world would be able to see things in the future to some extent. Therefore, this could sometimes work as an approach to prove the existence of the other world.

For example, you might have a gut feeling or hunch, which might somehow cause you to think, "That person is likely to pass away soon," and then they really do. On another occasion, you might feel, "Something good is going to happen soon," and it does. Through experiences like these, people may come to know a world other than this one.

In that sense, foresight can also work as a catalyst to attract people to the spiritual world. It is one of the most useful aspects of foresight.

6

Astral Projection

To close this chapter, I would like to include astral projection.

Astral projection is an out-of-body experience in which the soul separates from the body and is able to wander in the other world. It is sometimes referred to as teleportation.

Astral projection can, in a sense, be experienced by almost everyone. This is because we can visit the spiritual world during sleep. Using this as a premise, it can be said that nearly everyone might have experienced astral projection and has the potential to be a psychic.

Moreover, I would like to give some consideration to the question of whether astral projection is possible during waking hours when a person is conscious and aware, not limited to the period of sleep.

One of the most noted practitioners of this ability was Emanuel Swedenborg, a Swedish psychic. He is said to have locked himself in his room and lay prostrate almost as if dead for as long as a week at times, exploring the other world with his ability of astral projection.

However, it could have been a dangerous situation when his physical body was in a deathlike state. Even with the silver cord tethering his spirit to his body, his body was left empty, making it susceptible to be controlled by evil or malicious spirits while in that state. This is the reason that astral projection can involve great danger.

Therefore, in order to perform astral projection frequently, one needs the support of one's own guardian and guiding spirits. Without their protection, there is extreme peril.

Nonetheless, astral projection can usually become possible after you have developed a certain level of spiritual ability. One of the conditions that can make it possible is that you are able to set aside time daily to ensure moments of peace. This is essential. You need time without any interruption from others, time without interference. Without this condition, astral projection is not possible.

In modern times, it is almost impossible to find any time for serenity or for a pause without interference from others. Most of us in this age are constantly busy at work or having interactions with other people.

So it is logical to think that it would be easier to practice astral projection while meditating in a mountain retreat as was done in ancient times,

Now, what exactly happens when astral projections take place?

In most cases, you will be able to experience astral projection while in meditation. As you leave your body, you will be able to look down on it below you. Your body could be seen as similar to the shell of a cicada that has been shed. It is the experience of being able to look at another you.

Just like normal sight, you will be able to clearly see the room and all the things in it. Gradually, your body rises higher and higher, passing through the ceiling of the room and further through the roof, eventually rising above the building you are in. If it is nighttime, you will be able to see the stars spreading across the sky. If it is daytime, you can see the layout of houses and into the distance. In this way, you may roam from place to place.

It is also possible to instantly travel to a foreign location if you have a sense of purpose for your astral projection. You can go to China, Russia, or the United States while your physical body is in Japan.

There are also forms of astral projection other than your soul leaving your body. One of them is the focusing of your will outside your body. This is an ability that is very similar to the mystical power of *kanjizai*.

While sitting in meditation and attempting to search for something far away, perhaps some foreign site, you may be able to actually view it. During this time, your condition will be that you are still in your body but also out of your body. It is your will that enables you to see the world far away. There is such a state.

This is also a form of astral projection in which a part of the soul inhabiting a physical body leaves the body and travels to observe distant places. In other words, it is possible, while seated at rest, to have an astral projection and see and sense things that are far away.

There is also a special form of astral projection called the phenomenon of materialization.

In such a case, it is possible for a spirit that has left the body to materialize in a totally different location appearing in ordinary human form or even manifest in multiple places simultaneously. Since ancient times, there have been many Indian hermit yogis who have had this ability. Many people can actually make their spiritual forms materialize not only in one place, but elsewhere as well.

Therefore, many different capabilities exist, but you need to know that astral projection is just a part of the total experience. In other words, it is only one way to observe the extraordinary Spirit World. I think that astral projection is just one aspect of spiritual phenomena, and it is not so important in itself.

The most important keys would be to establish a system of theories to explain the true state of the Spirit World and provide written proof of that world. I believe those to be the most essential matters, and that the occurrence of phenomena are only incidental or additional.

In this chapter, I have explained various kinds of spiritual abilities.

In conclusion, I would say that spiritual abilities are expedient and serve as clues to inform people about the real world. In this sense, they are meaningful. On the other hand, it is also true that there are risks involved when dealing with them, as you may have learned from experience.

Therefore, if you are a person on some kind of mission and have the spiritual ability, you must use it very carefully. You have to live your life doing work with the utmost effort while maintaining a humble attitude. You also need to be mindful of living a lifestyle that would be a good example to many others. Only then would you be able to make use of your spiritual abilities.

This attitude would lead to *rojin*, the mystical power, which I will discuss in the next chapter.

Chapter 4

Rojin,
the Mystical Power

1

Shakyamuni Buddha's Teachings

In this chapter, I would like to discuss the topic of *rojin*, the main subject of this book.

First, I want to point out that the *rojin*, the mystical power, originates from the teachings of Shakyamuni Buddha, or Gautama Siddhartha, who was active in India nearly 2,600 years ago. Many of you may already know that his teachings are called Buddhism.

Embedded in the roots of Shakyamuni Buddha's teachings was the concept of self-establishment. It is based on the following idea: "The reason for our existence on earth is to use our environment as material for study to improve our souls. Unless each individual learns from their surrounding circumstances, life on earth will be meaningless."

This clearly shows that the Buddha's teachings are based on each individual's power to be self-reliant. From the beginning, he never taught that salvation could be achieved just by calling out the name of God or any other power. Shakyamuni's teachings essentially centered on improving oneself first.

This idea can be symbolized by the self-generation of one's inner light. "Let the light shine on you, and kindle your own inner torch. Do not ask for anyone's help, but grow brighter by your own light," taught the Buddha. This idea can be expressed as self-illumination.

Simultaneously, he taught the idea of lighting up from within using the torch of Dharma. "After I pass away, you should live your life based on the Dharma that I have preached, abiding by it. You should not rely on others, but live your lives according to the Dharma," was the message he taught at the end of his life on earth. This idea is called the Dharma light. This tenet of lighting up one's inner light and living according to the Dharma light is one of the fundamental teachings of Shakyamuni Buddha.

One might question, "Why did Shakyamuni think of and teach the idea of improving oneself?" It is because, ultimately, this would lead to progress for the entire universe created by God. "Each individual must learn and improve from one's place while ensuring one's own footing." Shakyamuni taught that this idea would lead to the betterment of the whole universe.

Therefore, it is certain that at the root of Shakyamuni Buddha's teachings was no thought of changing the world through prayer alone. He placed great importance on the idea of self-reflection to enable individual advancement. This idea can also be expressed as "benefitting oneself leads to benefitting others." The idea is that when one lives a life that is beneficial to oneself, this will enable doing good to others at the same time.

If you look at the phrase "benefit yourself," the word "benefit" may not immediately portray its intended meaning, but it is the idea of "aiming for the betterment of others as you pursue your own path of improvement." If understood superficially, it may seem egotistical, but it is not intended to suggest that you should be selfish.

Ideas such as "I will perish in order for others to be saved," or "My self-sacrifice is the only way for others to survive" may sound glorious, but these phrases involve tragic endings. Although forms of self-sacrifice may appear in various evolutions of the Truth being spread, they would still not lead to creating greater harmony, or to further progress.

Basic to Shakyamuni Buddha's teachings was the idea that "Each human being must improve themself. In the process of improvement, they must seek ways to help others progress without harming them." It is precisely because of this way of thinking that Buddhism has achieved great development since then.

The foundation of Buddhism is the mindset of tolerance. The attribute of tolerance will enable positivity for the progress of all things. One must be in control of oneself, correct one's own mistakes, and strive to improve. At the same time, it is necessary to consider the progress of others without harming them. By holding strongly to the values expressed in the Middle Way, everything and everyone will be allowed to progress. Then, each person will respect one another's viewpoints in tolerance of one another.

Now, let us consider spiritual abilities based on Shakyamuni Buddha's teachings. If we note the attitude of present-day psychics, we can see that most of them have come to have corrupted, dangerous beliefs of their psychic abilities.

What would be the danger of such beliefs? It would be like holding an unsheathed sword in one's hands; holding such an instrument and not knowing how to use it would be trouble.

Similarly, the use of psychic abilities can harm others but also cause harm to oneself if used inappropriately.

Despite this fact, it seems that many psychics only wish to show off their psychic abilities as if wielding a sword.

Comparing this activity to those of Shakyamuni Buddha's teachings – that benefiting the self can benefit others or the ideas of the torch within and the torch of Dharma – you would find a great difference between them. In the case of common psychics, their having spiritual abilities would not lead others to grow, and using the abilities may even lead to their own ruin. Such great danger is present.

In contrast, Shakyamuni Buddha possessed all of the six divine or mystical powers*, but in normal circumstances, he chose to keep them hidden, purposely not revealing them to the public. You cannot usually tell the difference between a person who has chosen not to display any mystical powers they possess and another who does not have them. However, the difference in terms of implication is significant, and you need to be aware of this crucial point.

We can find an indication of Shakyamuni Buddha's teachings in his practice of keeping his inner power hidden, being discreet

---

* The six divine powers:

The supernatural powers unique to the Buddha (the enlightened one) are: *tengen* (the ability to see spiritually; spiritual sight), *ten'ni* (the ability to hear the voices of spirits; spiritual hearing), *tashin* (the ability to understand a person's thoughts as if they were one's own), *shukumyo* (the ability to know one's future or a person's destiny), *jinsoku* (ability of astral projection), and *rojin* (the ability to transcend worldly desires without being swayed by them).

in his manner; he conscientiously kept his accumulated powers in store. Moreover, instead of letting his light rush out blindly, he controlled the intensity of the light to inspire people. Instead of giving out overwhelming light, he influenced people with subdued light. Shakyamuni was deliberate in gradually influencing people with a light that would not hurt their eyes.

Thus, common manifestations of psychic powers may exhibit light like bright glaring reflections in a mirror or from a glass sculpture that can be harmful to the eyes of onlookers and may even damage the psychic's own eyes. There is such danger involved.

On the other hand, teaching and influencing people with a steady, low-intensity light instead of a blazing light requires a great deal of endurance, patience, and perseverance.

However, it can be said that although it requires patience, this is the path to great progress and a higher level of perfection.

It is a mistake to have tendencies of showing off one's abilities, making pretensions, seeking people's attention, or becoming self-exalted. You must be wary of these kinds of attitudes. You must not act in a manner that would regularly aggravate the feelings of other people by frightening or intimidating them with a show of threatening behavior.

You cannot seek Truth with acts that would alarm or cause dismay in others. Instead, aim to establish yourself firmly by building up strength within yourself. Rather than overwhelming others with your power all at once, aim to influence people with light that is given out little by little. In this way, you will be directed toward a life in which you will influence and educate people without causing them excessive irritation or losing your own footing.

From this point on, I believe that we must seriously consider the path of human perfection and educating others, which takes decades to achieve. Do not simply show off your spiritual abilities for the sake of immediate self-gratification, a gain in temporary reputation, or short-lived popularity. This is my very strong desire.

2

The Behaviors of Psychics in the Modern Age

Keeping the above explanations in mind, I would like to reconsider the behavior of modern psychics.

What are modern psychics like? To say the least, I think it is true that most of them are not respected by the people of the world. While they may not gain much respect in the world, quite a number of them are able to stir people's interest. They seem to attract the attention and interest of young people by doing things that others cannot do.

For example, they may make such claims as: "You can change your destiny by practicing a certain set of disciplinary rules," "I can produce a dragon from a flame," "If you chant this prayer, everything will get better," "You will be prevented from any illness if you wear this charm," "Drinking this sacred water will instantly heal your illness," or "You will be guaranteed a place in heaven if you join this group," and so on. It seems many psychics make such statements as they perform their spiritual abilities in order to persuade others.

Indeed, spiritual abilities themselves are gifts from God, instruments to teach people the Truth, so spiritual abilities can be a way to teach, influence, and make many people aware of the Truth. However, if used to inappropriate extremes, spiritual abilities may not only disrupt the common sense of people but may also cause them to go astray.

Religion is something wonderful and should be appreciated by the world, but unfortunately, the word "religion" itself causes a negative reaction to people in modern Japan. I must say that this situation is worsened by the many psychics on the streets who are trying to take advantage of people. They are using various schemes to profit from deceiving people. They are a cause of confusion.

When I view the behavior of modern psychics, I feel that most of them do not possess *rojin*, the mystical power. This is the power that enables one to live as a normal, reasonable person, while in actuality they deserve greater respect as a person who possesses spiritual abilities.

Many unusual people can be found, especially among the crowd of claimants professing to have heard the voice of God or that of a high spirit. I feel strongly that this type of situation should be rectified. This situation should not continue; it must be changed no matter the difficulty. There is an urgent need to reform the image and behavior of such a hodgepodge of psychics.

There is a serious problem in this earthly world, it is that there is no standard for judging what is right and what is wrong, what is true and what is false, regarding spiritual abilities.

One of the reasons why I have been consecutively displaying spiritual phenomena and publishing books of spiritual messages is because I am attempting to create a standard of measurement. Of course, the fact that different psychics demonstrate different phenomena or teachings can be seen as a reflection of the individuality and different facets of the diverse personalities of the high spirits. On the other hand, by publishing books of spiritual messages, I am attempting to ask, "Is the particular psychic displaying a feature that can be seen as part of the vast array of rightful teachings or something completely inappropriate?"

I must say that the biggest problem with modern psychics is that they are likely to give their followers misguided teaching and let them practice the wrong principles of spiritual discipline. Many of the followers and disciples are being led to an undesirable realm. Another problem is that the followers can be misguided into the worship of spiritual abilities, thinking that the possession of spiritual abilities is meaningful in itself. This is truly distressing. You must not be trapped by the worship of spiritual abilities.

In fact, from the perspective of one who is able to observe spiritual beings, those who call themselves gods, Buddha, or high spirits often turn out to be nothing more than animal spirits. Humans, supposedly the pinnacle of creation with the highest intelligence, are at the mercy of foxes wagging their tails, or snakes and other animal spirits. This kind of stupidity actually occurs.

Human beings must have more dignity. In order to regain your dignity, you need to accurately grasp the world of Truth. You have to know what is and what is not the Truth.

You have to be aware that ignorance is a sin. Because of ignorance, you can live as if nothing is wrong. Isn't that the way the majority of people are today? They assume that not knowing about the Spirit World is not a problem. They take ignorance for granted. On the other hand, when it comes to people who are aware of spiritual matters, they are regarded as crazy. These kinds of common beliefs have to be refuted somehow.

We need to show that there are wonderful things in the spiritual world, and by working to let the light shine through from those wonderful things, we can clearly show how much evil forces are lurking in this world. When the sun shines on them, wrongdoers will be driven away. There is simply not enough sunlight. I feel there is a much greater need to make the sunlight more powerful for divine benefit than to worry about cleaning up the pestilence.

Our position, then, is to never deny spiritual abilities. Instead, I would like people with spiritual abilities to build greater, more wonderful characters, to have more outstanding power, and to live in ways that earn the respect of more people. This is how I want such people to be. Shouldn't this be the way a psychic should be in the modern day?

Setting aside any claims of "God said..." "Buddha said..." or, the "high spirits said...," there should be the accountability of your thoughts, words, actions, beliefs, ideas, and past history; these are things that you should not regret if presented to the world. You would be challenged by such a personal inspection. You need to make sure that you are not ashamed of your past record. I would not approve if you were to claim, "I suddenly attained enlightenment in a state of total insanity," or "I suddenly heard God's voice after decades of living in despair," or "I heard God's voice when falling off a cliff." I do not believe anyone would be shown the path of Truth in these situations.

If God really sent his own only begotten son or anyone close to Him to this earth, they would have to have superlative abilities in a worldly sense, too. Otherwise, it would not be possible that they would qualify as a supreme guiding spirit in the heavenly realm; they must also possess relevant abilities in the worldly sense. That is what I can say.

Therefore, a key question is whether one is considered exceptional simply as a person, setting aside any spiritual ability such as being able to hear the voice of God. At the very least, if one is not considered an above-average person in the human sense, then having a spiritual ability will only be a negative attribute. Such an ability would only work negatively. It would be questioned whether one is an above-average person, with a desirable caliber of character, even without spiritual abilities. This is an important point.

Thus, the behavior of modern psychics must be measured putting aside any spiritual power they may have. It would be desirable that a person of excellent stature would be able to double, triple, or quadruple the strength of their abilities by having spiritual abilities. They must not expect the spirits to do everything for them and eventually fall under sway of these spirits' influence. This is something I strongly believe.

3

Overcoming Bad Aspects of Mediumship Embodiment

Continuing on the topic of modern psychics, I would like to talk about overcoming detrimental aspects of mediumship.

Doing away with negativity should be a call for awareness to all psychics. All psychics have some form of mediumship embodiment. There are various types of spiritual abilities: spiritual sight, spiritual speech, spiritual hearing, the ability of foresight, and so on. All of these are related to mediumship, the ability to communicate with spirits.

What does it mean to be a medium? It is to have the power to invite spirits to possess one's physical body. Actually, it is an ability that all humans share. Shakyamuni Buddha, Jesus Christ, and Moses were all mediums in their own particular way. As mediums, they were able to use their physical bodies as sources of spiritual power.

The ability to use one's physical body as an instrument for spiritual communication means that the mind in control of that body is capable of emitting unique wavelengths that correspond to a spirit. The body itself does not have much significance in this activity. The mind in control of the body has the power to connect spiritually while it is still in harmony with the body – this would describe the state of a person when performing an act of a medium.

However, there are two types of mediums: high-level mediums and low-level or demonic mediums. Actually, more than 90% of the world's spiritual communicators are low-grade mediums being linked to spirits of a demonic nature. It is often the case that those people are influenced by evil spirits and serving their will.

Once you have become a low-level medium, you will then have difficulty ridding yourself of such spirits, no matter how hard you try. Unexpectedly, you may start to hear strange voices or a particular spirit may enter you and cause your body to move; it would become impossible to overcome these situations.

As you begin to hear the voices whispering in your ears, you might hear them saying, "Get in the car today," or "Go to such and such a place today." If you follow these voices, they will lead you to much trouble. They may say things like, "You'll have an accident sooner or later," or "Your company will go bankrupt," or even worse, "Put this electric cord around your neck," or "Throw all your money around town," or some other strange things. They may even ask you to buy fresh fish for them, or they may ask you to serve some particular food. This is what happens.

When you hear the command of a spiritual being, would you really believe that it is the voice of God? Could you believe that it is the voice of a high spirit? You have to judge this carefully. If it is a high spirit, it should have lived a former life as a superior person on earth. You have to ask yourself, "Would such a superior being say such things when they return to the other world?"

In the history of mankind, spiritual leaders such as Shakyamuni Buddha, Christ, or Moses, and in Japan, priests such as Kukai, Nichiren, and Shinran were people with extraordinary natures; they had highly refined thoughts and excellent characters. Would they say such odd things after leaving the earthly life to return to the other world? We need to think about this. In principle, it would not make sense.

So, how would it be possible for a person who is a low-grade medium to break free of the dreadful situation that they are trapped in? Let us look at measures that would provide a cure.

The first solution is to utterly ignore low-level spirits. No matter what these spirits whisper, comment, or do, they must be ignored. This attitude should be maintained for at least a year. As you do this, you will eventually develop a constitution that will keep spirits from haunting you. This attitude of completely shutting them out and never responding to them is important.

If you comply to the suggestions of the voices you hear, following them with no control over your own arms and legs, you will eventually become a completely controlled puppet of low-level spirits. Instead, totally reject them by firmly establishing your own independent will. It is very important to stand on your own. This is one way to break free of low-level spirits. These spirits are seeking individuals to talk to, so they will never approach anyone who will not listen to them. This is what you should consider first.

Another solution is to align your mind to the teachings of the books of Truth, making it a custom to read such books every day. In other words, by spending a certain amount of time reading a book that is full of light, you will allow the light to constantly fill your mind. You need to let brilliant light shine into your mind. This would provide you with a method to remain untroubled by any spiritual disturbance. As the light shines into you, your nature will change to have an affinity with high spirits. This is how you could stop receiving vibrations from lower spirits.

Besides reading books, you can also listen to CDs of lectures on the Truth. In this way, you would be able to listen to the voices of guiding spirits of light in person. Listening to them would change your vibrations, the wavelengths of your mind so that you will be attuned to the high spirits. These are actions you should take. As you continue your efforts, evil thoughts that linger in your mind will gradually be dispelled, breaking the stronghold of low-level spirits within you.

Thus, there are such methods as ignoring bad spirits, reading books of Truth, and listening to lectures of Truth. There is yet another method, making efforts to establish yourself as a respectable person in this world.

Each person should be engaged in some kind of work. If you are working, there is a way to exert yourself to the highest degree within your position, making a wholehearted effort at work, living your life in the best way possible. If you are a housewife, strive to be the best housewife you can be. If you are a salesperson, strive to be the best salesperson you can be. If you are a business executive, strive to be the best business executive you can be. In this way, with all your energy, devote your efforts to doing what you feel is valuable and provides you a livelihood. This is another way to free yourself from the negative aspects of mediumship.

Indeed, it is characteristic of people that they cannot think of two things at the same time. This means that if you are dealing with low-level spirits you have idle time available to become involved. It also means that you have placed yourself in an environment where it is possible for you to interact with these spirits. Therefore, in order to break free from any involvement with them, it is important to put all your energy into meaningful work, even though it may sound rather worldly.

The fourth method to overcome damaging mediumship is to remain healthy. It is very important to maintain good health and physical fitness. When you feel weak or are in poor health, it would be very difficult to escape from adverse mediumship. Therefore, it is important to focus on building a healthy body first. A healthy way of life with a healthy body is essential.

As in the old saying, "A sound mind dwells in a sound body," a sound body would cause spirits of higher levels to come in response. Evil spirits are less likely to haunt a person who has a strong and healthy body. Conversely, they are usually attracted to people who are constantly in a state of mental distress or who complain of some physical illness. They can be people who suffer from some kind of neurosis or internal organ ailment. These people become easy prey to evil spirits.

Therefore, to overcome the negative effects of low-grade mediumship, it is necessary to strengthen your physical body. By doing this, your soul will become stronger.

The fifth and the last method I must mention is to strengthen your will, the power to control your mind. What exactly is the will? In other words, it is the gift you have been given as a child of God. This is what you need to fortify.

Be aware that you are a child of God. Have strong awareness that you are alive devoting yourself to the creation of utopia on earth. It is a strong awareness that you are not a person at the mercy of fate, but a powerful person living to fulfill God's intent. It is confidence, and confidence and awareness will protect you from evil spirits. I think these realizations are very important.

4

Kanjizai

I have talked about low-level mediumship, but in contrast, among the abilities of high-level mediumship, there is an ability called *kanjizai*, and I would like to talk a little about this.

The Heart Sutra of Buddhism starts with the phrase, "Aryavalokitesvaro bodhisattvo gambhiram prajnaparamita caryam caramano vyavalokayati," which translates as, "when Kanjizai bodhisattva has deepened his state of spiritual training and has accessed the treasure of the inner subconscious." Kanjizai bodhisattva is Avalokitesvara, an ancient Indian term. It means "a person having the state of mind of a bodhisattva, who understands all things clearly as if they were a part of his or her own thoughts."

The first aspect of *kanjizai*, the mystical power, is to be able to understand the thoughts of others as if they were one's own. This stage is known by the term *tashin*, one of the six divine powers. *Tashin* is the ability to understand the minds of others, the so-called mind-reading ability. In other words, it is to be able to read what is inside the minds of other people. It is often cited as one of the most important aspects of *kanjizai*.

With this ability, when you are giving lectures before large groups, you can grasp the thoughts inside the minds of the people in attendance. You would be able to comprehend who is sitting before you, and what he or she is thinking. With the ability of *tashin*, you can perform this feat unconsciously.

The ability to read people's thoughts clearly was one of the most conspicuous ones that Shakyamuni Buddha possessed. This ability would be strengthened when a person is placed in a relevant position where this ability is required. In other words, as one is fulfilling the responsibilities of leading others, this ability will be further enhanced. It could be said that this would be proof of Truth and that the person had been sent down by God. Thus, this would be the initial aspect of *kanjizai*.

Another aspect of *kanjizai* is the power to see the three phases of existence of a person – their past, present, and future. It is the ability to look into and read the past lives of people.

What kind of life did a particular person lead in the past? It is the ability to see deeply into the past history of this person, not only the past within their current life, but also their past existence, and the ones before that, and so on. Where did the person live, what kind of life did he or she live, and what were their feelings when they died? What characteristics have they acquired from past lives? What strengths have they gained and what weaknesses have they created? What kinds of relationships have they been blessed with? With the ability to read past lives, one would be able to comprehend such things.

Yet another aspect of *kanjizai* is the ability to see the future, which can be called foresight. It means to be able to see the future lives of people, or comprehend what will happen in the future.

When Shakyamuni Buddha was about to leave the earthly world more than 2,500 years ago, he said, "I will later be reincarnated in Kentumati of Jambudvipa." In modern translation, Kentumati of Jamdvipa means a great city of an Eastern country. With that prediction, he passed away.

He also stated, "My Dharma will eventually spread to all of India, and then will be passed on to China, and from China to Japan. After my passing, the Age of the Right Dharma will continue for 500 years. But for the 500 years after that, the Age of the Semblance Dharma will continue. The Age of Right Dharma would be the time when the teachings are correctly transmitted and people's minds would hold correct thoughts. However, in the Age of Semblance Dharma, only the form will remain, and the content will gradually become diminished. After that will follow the Age of the Latter Day of the Dharma. The Dharma will fade away." This is what Shakyamuni Buddha said.

There are currently different ideas regarding the periods of time being referred to, whether they are 500 years, 800 years, or 1,000 years, but there is general agreement that there are different stages.

"There will be a time when the Right Dharma is spread to others, a time when it will become only a formality, and a time when it will eventually become obsolete. In the Latter Day of the Dharma, the true Buddha will be reincarnated and provide new teachings." This is what Shakyamuni Buddha predicted.

This future Buddha was to be called Maitreya Bodhisattva in the ancient Indian language. Thus a prediction of the future was told.

Such a prophecy to predict the future and the ability to observe the three phases of human existence – past, present, and future – were significant abilities of Shakyamuni Buddha.

There is another aspect of *kanjizai*, the ability to read the minds of people in distant places as if their thoughts were one's own. This is the ability to know the thoughts and feelings of people who are not physically present, but in some far-off place hundreds or thousands of kilometers away. Furthermore, solutions would be provided for their concerns with suggestions like, "There is a person in such and such a place that you should go and see. At that place, there will be such and such an outcome." It is the ability to spiritually see distant places and read the minds of people there.

Thus, the level of the mystical power of *kanjizai* is considerably high. It is similar to the level of enlightenment of the Brahma Realm and can extend higher into the Tathagata Realm. These mystical powers can be described as a part of one's psychic constitution and would be manifested naturally by those who possess them.

This is true not only on earth but also in the heavenly realms. Spirits have different degrees of *kanjizai* depending on which level they are situated, but this does not mean a spirit in the other world would know everything. Oppositely, spirits who are lost in the realm of hell would not comprehend much at all.

The spirits that have returned to the heavenly realms are able to understand many things to varying degrees. The higher the dimension, the more things they could take in and comprehend. This is the true nature of things.

Therefore, you could say that there are no bounds to the mystical power of *kanjizai*. When one reaches the final stage of *kanjizai*, one will have the ability to instantly grasp everything that is happening on earth; as the old saying goes, "God is aware of a single leaf as it falls to the ground." At the ultimate stage of *kanjizai*, one will reach a point where one can understand everything about the Great Universe. This is how the mystical power of *kanjizai* can be described.

5

The Extraordinary in the Ordinary

A person who lives while embodying the mystical power of *kanjizai* would stand out from others. Often, because of these extraordinary abilities, one might be tempted to boast about them. However, if one blurted out something about another person's future or past, or what that person was currently thinking, the one making such statements would likely be categorized as eccentric and strange by others. Then, unfortunately, one would reluctantly have to live life with this unfavorable reputation.

Therefore, even if you are the embodiment of a high spirit or possess the mystical power of *kanjizai*, you must be sure to realize that you are living as a person of this world. This is necessary. The efforts you are expected to make to confirm your life can be expressed in the phrase "extraordinary in the ordinary."

If you consider yourself to be outstanding and different from everyone else, this notion could lead you to form an extreme personality that would appear bizarre and abnormal in the eyes of others. Instead, you should try to manifest the "extraordinary in the ordinary." While living an ordinary life no different from that of ordinary people, you could quietly nurture the seeds of your abilities and use them conscientiously. This would align with the attitude of exerting oneself in an unpretentious manner.

People who want to be successful are often obsessed with a desire for self-display. They often become preoccupied with such concerns as how to look good, appeal to people, and get a good reputation. They increasingly become more abnormal and experience intense waves of both good and bad. This is not desirable.

In practicing the extraordinary in the ordinary, it is important to shine an extraordinary light into ordinary life in times that seem to flow quietly and continuously. As you do the same things ordinary people do, it is important to let others know that common activities can be done in a remarkable manner.

Being extraordinary in the ordinary is what you should be proud of. If you are apparently exceptional, it might seem to follow naturally that you would live an incredible life, but that should not be the consequence. It is more important to leave behind the shimmer of your soul, a glowing light while living a quite ordinary life like everyone else. I sincerely hope that you will cherish this idea.

Do not seek the extraordinary for its own sake. Even if you pursue the extraordinary, it would be a solitary experience limited to your personal experience and could not be used as an example for others to try. It is rather more important to increase the brilliance of one's soul and emit more light in a way of life that others could emulate.

So what exactly is the extraordinary in the ordinary? Let us consider a business environment. People who work in the business world have ethics but do not usually like to reveal their religious beliefs. They do not want to be bound by religious beliefs or to talk about them. They would rather pretend to show that they do not care much about such things. Sure, that is fine. In the workplace or during business dealings, people who constantly proclaim their love of God or Buddha would be considered bizarre or out of place. That is not how it should be. Do not practice the extraordinary in that sense.

I would like you to work in a proper manner. As you fulfill your work duties, you should show the light you have accumulated through the learning of Truth.

You do not need to mention the name of God or Buddha, nor do you need to talk about any spiritual beings, such as high spirits or your own guardian spirit. You should just be one who shows kindness and explores ways to be a better human being. Explore the wonderment of how the mind works and what it can do. Aim to be one who leads people by influencing them with your example. Aim to be a person like that.

6

The Ultimate Attainment of the Mystical Power of *Rojin*

To close this chapter, I would like to talk about the ultimate attainment of the mystical power of *rojin*.

Rojin is considered the greatest of the six divine powers possessed by Shakyamuni Buddha. It is the ability to exercise spiritual abilities to the highest degree while living a life that is considered most superior in the worldly sense. How can one achieve this ultimate level?

If a living person wants to master the mystical power of *rojin*, it is essential to raise one's awareness. In other words, you need to have the same level of awareness as the high spirits, even though you are living in human form. Not only should you accept the revelations of high spirits as their teachings, but you also need to understand the outline, level, breadth, and distinct characteristics of the teachings they intend to spread.

Therefore, the ultimate attainment of the mystical power of *rojin* can be explained as being able to comprehend the very essence of spiritual phenomena without being affected by them. Upon hearing the words of different high spirits, if a person could instantly perceive the differences in their personalities, the quality of their teachings, or whether their teachings were superior or inferior, it would be very easy for such a person to live in this world. With that ability, one could then clearly understand the differences in the ways of thinking and consciousnesses of people living on earth. Consequently, one would know how to bring each different spiritual idea into reality.

Based on these abilities, teaching each person in a personalized manner becomes possible. Among Shakyamuni Buddha's teachings, it is said that preaching a sermon that best suits each person's tendencies and capabilities is particularly important. It has often been noted that he "taught in a way that suited each person," that he "taught according to each person's nature," and that "his own character transformed to save different people." Depending on who he was dealing with, the way he taught others varied; his teachings were modified in terms of level, breadth, and content. At one time he might have said one thing, and another time he might have said something that sounded completely different. What he said to one person might be expressed from a different perspective when speaking to another person.

Therefore, those who received teachings would not necessarily understand the true intentions of Shakyamuni Buddha. That is what has been said of his teachings, and this happened because he possessed the ability to preach in a personalized manner, according to each person's abilities and circumstances.

The source of this ability is found in the fact that he could completely understand the thoughts and minds of all human beings. To be able to understand the minds and thoughts of all people meant that he could fully comprehend all of the divided rays of light that were teachings emanating from God as the source of all. His ability was based on the fact that he knew every hue of light as each of the many facets of God.

After all, Shakyamuni Buddha's confidence in giving sermons according to each person's abilities and circumstances was based on his ability to analyze even the teachings of high spirits as he listened to them. His source of power was found there.

He was capable of critically examining the teachings and thoughts of any spirit while he was alive. With such an ability, it was easy for him to identify evil spirits, demons, or devils, not just the high spirits. He could quite easily determine their true nature.

In order to fathom the true nature of devils, it is particularly important that you are not affected by any desire. If you are obsessed with desires, you will not be able to see the evil spirits for what they are. In contrast, if you remain detached from any desire and live with a serenity like the undisturbed flow of water, you will be able to see into the spiritual nature of such beings.

Therefore, in comprehending the thoughts of various spirits, the way to recognize the thoughts of evil spirits, in particular, is to live each day with serenity and in a detached manner. You should not allow yourself to become emotionally irritated. When you find your feelings becoming agitated, focus your effort to adjust them as quickly as possible to restore tranquility within your mind.

Serenity within is essential. To avoid being possessed by evil spirits or to ward off their control, it is important to have a mind at peace, a mind that can immediately return to calmness no matter what happens. Without such a state of mind, the ability to perceive spiritual essence will not be attained.

On the other hand, to be able to communicate properly with high spirits, you need to refine your soul in a suitable manner. To do this, because you have been incarnated on earth, you also need to learn things in a worldly sense.

When it comes to learning, you can certainly gain knowledge from books and other sources. You can also learn through contact with different types of people. You also need to consider how to provide nourishment for your soul and be aware of the life lessons in all that you have experienced.

Over time, the reason why high spirits have been able to obtain skillful insight and perception is that they have learned lessons and gained gems of wisdom from their many experiences, and have surrounded themselves with the light they have gained. To approach the state of mind of the high spirits, people on earth should also gain the light that shines like gems from things they have experienced on earth and envelop themselves in it.

How much nourishment for the soul do we draw from our daily lives, day in and day out? This is essential. For all people, one day is only twenty-four hours long. What could we learn in those twenty-four hours? What valuable lessons could be extracted in that time? This would be the source of wisdom. If you are able to distill the same kind of wisdom from your daily life as the high spirits have done, you will also be able to say that you are on the same level as they are.

The disciplinary goal for people should be to attain this level, to be able to understand the minds of all spirits and all human beings and match your communicative ability to suit each of them. By doing so, you will be able to improve yourself as an educator, as a leader. It is only when you have reached such a state that you can attain the ultimate level of *rojin*, the mystical power. To attain this ultimate level should be the highest goal of spiritual discipline in this world. This is how I see it.

Chapter 5

Buddha's Truth and
Its Study

1

The Importance of Studying

At Happy Science, we value highly the exploration and study of Buddha's Truth. Regarding Buddha's Truth, I would like to state that exploration comes before study, and study comes before missionary work. We should not alter the order of exploration, study, and conveying the Truth; otherwise, we cannot expect the Truth to be spread in the right way. The three stages of exploration, study, and conveying the Truth are very important.

Primarily, I believe most endeavors to explore the Truth to be mainly the work of a religious teacher, although it is also possible to explore the Truth on an individual basis. Therefore, in normal situations, people should focus on how to study the results of the exploration of Truth. Here, I would like to emphasize the importance of studying the Truth.

Why would it be important to study Buddha's Truth? I will now discuss this point in more detail.

The reason why the study of Buddha's Truth is so important is that it helps to build a deep understanding of the criteria for the evaluation of things. From birth into adulthood, what we have learned in school, from our friends, and from our parents form the foundation of our perceptions and judgment. Outside of this social environment, there is very little we absorb from other sources. I would say that what these sources most probably consider to be common sense or knowledge is often very worldly.

Accordingly, it is highly unlikely that most people would be aware of the higher level of perception, or Buddha's Truth. If your parents grew up in a deeply religious environment, or are actually engaged in such related vocations, or have a general interest in religious matters, you would be fortunate, but in most situations, this is not the case.

In this sense, it could be said that you would not be able to comprehend or grasp the essence of Buddha's Truth unless you were to begin studying it.

Then, why does the study of Buddha's Truth have value? Let me discuss this topic.

It is because Buddha's Truth provides people with three truths. The Truth of God or Buddha teaches three truths.

The first truth gives the answer to: "What does it mean to be human? What is a human being?" It has long been the subject of much literature, art, philosophy, and thinking to pursue the answer to this. Not only in the studies of humanities, but also research in the fields of medicine, biology, and other sciences has been done to explore the question, "What is a human being?"

Since ancient times the mystery of "What is a human being?" has been repeatedly asked but has never been fully answered. Knowledge of Buddha's Truth is required to answer this fundamental question.

To know what it is to be human is, in a sense, to decipher why humans have life. We are now faced with, "Is a person alive just by chance?" "Were human beings thrown into the world by coincidence; are we just living randomly and by chance?" Thus, understanding what it means to be human is ultimately the key to solving the mystery of life. When we understand the true nature of a human being, we will begin to see what human life is. It means that we cannot understand the lives of people without understanding what it is to be a human being.

In this way, Buddha's Truth can comprehensively answer the question, "What is a human being?" Buddha's Truth is the answer.

Secondly, the value of Buddha's Truth and its significance as an object of study is that it ultimately gives us a sense of direction. Noting the position of the Pole Star, people can know which way north is. The Pole Star remains fixed in place while all the other stars circle around it. Without it, it would be difficult to determine due north.

Thus, unless one is taught which direction to follow to realize progress, prosperity, and improvement for human beings, one will never know the way.

When you realize what improvement truly means to human beings, you may find that what you thought was improvement was actually corruption.

For example, a woman might fight for something thinking that it would improve the status of women, but it would actually lead to the degradation of humanity. If there was an error in a woman's understanding of true humanity causing her to act in a way that was contrary to the betterment of humankind, then degradation could occur.

In this way, Buddha's Truth serves as an important beacon to show people the direction or goal to head toward. Without it, we would not be able to make the trek through life. It may be that people would wander aimlessly, and though some people with an artistic nature might enjoy it, for most people a journey without a destination would be difficult to accept.

After all, a journey has an intended destination. You need a purpose for your trip and an itinerary that shows when you leave and when you return. That is a journey. When you travel, you need a destination. You need a direction. Buddha's Truth is very important as it gives a direction to follow.

The third essence of Buddha's Truth answers, "Why is it important to study Buddha's Truth?" The answer would be that "It is fundamental for enhancing happiness." We live our lives seeking what is good for ourselves. However, when each one of us thinks this way, it often results in hurting others, misunderstanding, or making one another suffer.

In the face of such circumstances, we are being asked what kind of life we should live to be happy, and what kinds of actions we should take to expand the "space of happiness." The question is what should we do to make the places we are living into spaces of happiness.

Suppose there is a person A, a person B, and a person C. They strive to live happily as individuals, but as each of them tries to seek their own happiness, they may end up hurting one another. It is also the role of Buddha's Truth to teach us how to cooperate with each other. The question arises, "How should these three people live so that they can realize happiness among themselves as a whole?"

As I said earlier, the second aspect of Buddha's Truth is to teach us how to improve ourselves by showing what direction to take, but the third aspect is about seeking the expansion of overall happiness. Creating such an expansive space of happiness is also the way of the Buddha's Truth. We need to answer the question, "How can we enhance not only individual happiness but also the happiness of the whole?" After all, happiness is something that every human being is looking for.

Ultimately, the importance of studying Buddha's Truth is based on these three points. The first is to answer the question, "What is a human being?" The second is to teach people the direction in which they should proceed. The third is to provide a basis for happiness or to teach how to live a happy life. These are of main importance. Thus, the three ideas of "being human," "seeking improvement," and "overall happiness" are keywords for studying Buddha's Truth.

2

The Nature of Knowledge

Concerning study, I would now like to talk about knowledge or intellectual power. In other words, we have to find "What is the essence of knowledge?"

I believe that people in Japan and other developed countries today are making great efforts to improve their knowledge. In doing this, a lot of sacrifices are being made. Most children spend nearly two decades learning in environments to increase their knowledge. At the latest, the period of learning starts from the time they start elementary school and continues until they graduate from university, or about sixteen years. For some, it starts as early as nursery school or kindergarten. So there is generally a learning period of almost twenty years. During this time, we are obligated to make efforts to improve our knowledge.

This is a common path of education in advanced countries, but the purpose of education itself may not be as clear as we might think. It is often said that the purpose of education is to "cultivate character and create individuals who can contribute to society," but this does not quite capture the essence of education itself.

The essence of education is ultimately to develop knowledge. Or, it could be described as exploring the nature of knowledge. Knowledge is the sum total of understanding that people have accumulated, or what will be created through mental aptitude.

Since the ancient time of Socrates, it has been said that love of knowledge is the essence of human nature. And this love of knowledge is what differentiates humans from animals. The understanding of this difference has been passed down and has been shown to hold true.

When we consider the knowledge of animals, those raised in captivity may indeed be capable of performing some tricks. However, these are behaviors that have been taught to them, and if we look at the practical application of their learned behavior, we can say that it would be very limited.

On the other hand, the knowledge that people have acquired through education may not be used directly but can be said to have applicability and potential for development. I believe that the essence of human knowledge lies in these aspects of applicability and potential for development.

Learning geography or history by memorizing specific things in high school or college may not achieve anything immediately. However, learning these subjects will give you a base to build on. By using what has been learned earlier, we can then build on our thoughts later on. This is an important point. Ultimately, I think it can be said that knowledge that is discovered and learned through education is the knowledge that serves as the building blocks for later thinking.

In this way, it could be said that our humanity is measured by how much we can think intellectually, or in other words, by our capacity to think abstractly or philosophically. I guess you could use the term "thinking speculatively" to describe this ability.

There are limits to what we can understand. There is a difference between the simple understanding of commonly occurring words, such as "pigeon," "bean," "baby," "train," and "airplane," which refer to visible objects, and the understanding of abstract words that are not visible. There is, after all, a difference in complexity.

I think the words "God" and "Buddha" are representative of these abstract words; perhaps a word like "spirit" is too. Since these words denote things that cannot be readily seen, we can only understand them abstractly. Therefore, one aspect of a person's spirituality can be measured by the extent to which they can understand abstract ideas.

In this sense, I think there is a difference in perception concerning works of art and literature as well. For example, some may depict a simple story, while others may demonstrate the sense of poetry. What is called a "world masterpiece" is usually thought-provoking. The thoughts of the artist or author have been put into it.

On the other hand, some books are practical guides or how-to books. Some books teach only how to do calculations. Other books teach only how to deal with tax matters or explain some scientific field, yet other books only follow formulas of chemical equations for experiments. It may not be accurate to say that these books do not affect our souls, but they contain very little that would stimulate our spirituality.

Books that impact our way of living contain some kind of "core," "aspiration," or "attitude that would improve humanity."

Thus, the nature of knowledge involves an aspect that is abstract and speculative. We might say that the more one is capable of understanding such an aspect, the more spiritual one becomes. However, I believe that some people, such as academics, who can only use abstract words but cannot make any substantive arguments to explain them, will at some point lose altitude on their trajectory of spiritual thought and revert back to where they started. There may be such occurrences, but in most cases, the degree of improvement of a person's soul can be measured by the elevation and exaltation of his or her ideas and arguments.

3

Intellectual Power as the Key to *Rojin*, the Mystical Power

Here, I would like to discuss the essence of knowledge and intellectual power in relation to *rojin*, the mystical power, the subject of this book.

First, I would like to say that there is a relationship between knowledge and spiritual or psychic abilities, but there have been many exceptions to this first premise. There have been many psychics in Japan since ancient times, and I think it was rare that the level of their intelligence was very high. They usually did not have much education but possessed pure hearts, enabling them at some point to hear the voice of a god, Buddha, or a high spirit leading them to become religious teachers.

However, this set of circumstances could have given rise to a problem. Among the voices that the early psychics thought were high spirits, there could have been other spirits from different levels, even the voices of demons mixed in. This kind of confusion would often cause commotion in society.

A common characteristic of low-level spirits or evil spirits is that they are unable to think in a logical and orderly manner. They live with emotional ups and downs, and because they lead such emotional lives, they are unable to be constructive or think things through in a logical manner. Because of this situation, it is important to have a certain level of intelligence in order to identify what could be the whispering of evil or low-level spirits.

However, another problem presents itself. Because of their knowledge or intellectual power, highly intelligent people tend to be obstinate, being very difficult to move emotionally. The starting point for a person to become involved in religion would be spiritual inspiration and spiritual sensitivity. People who have established themselves in academia are often very cautious and suspicious, which prevents them from entering the path of faith. As you can see, the result of academic studies has often been counterproductive to religious faith. Rather, historically speaking, it may be said that the more learned people were, the more they tended to deny things such as spirits, God, or Buddha. This is because worldly knowledge, or "shallow wisdom," has hindered their understanding of Buddha's Truth.

From this point of view, it could be said that the chance of finding a person with both psychic abilities and great intellectual power was extremely rare.

However, if we look at the abilities of modern psychics, we can say that the great psychics were also very intelligent. This has been the case with Japanese psychics such as Onisaburo Deguchi [1871–1948, founder of the Omoto religious movement] and Masaharu Taniguchi [1893–1985, founder of Seicho-no-Ie]. I think it can be said that these great spiritualists of recent times were also very intellectually advanced. Although he may not have been a psychic, the famous Japanese religious leader Kanzo Uchimura [1861–1930, Christian evangelist] was also highly intelligent.

Thus, it could be said that in order to tell right from wrong and to explain the vague and ambiguous spiritual world in a way that can be understood by people in this world, we need an intellectual framework or an intellectual filter.

Considering how many people will understand and think about Buddha's Truth when I teach it in the future, I think it will be extremely important to provide teaching in a way that people would accept. So what would it be that most people in the world will accept? Primarily, in order to convince people, the teaching should not be ominous; it should not cause fear; it should not be too outrageous.

The majority of Japanese people are highly educated. Since their intellectual level is so high, people will not be moved or find happiness in learning unless the content of the Buddha's Truth is also of a considerably high level. In this sense, the content should minimally exceed the average intellectual level of society.

I would also like to point out that intellectual power has yet another implication.

Even people with advanced spiritual abilities can get caught up in the whirlwind of spiritual phenomena as they live day by day. They may not be able to tell whether an event that is happening is in the spirit world, an illusion, or only their own circumstances.

As they hear the stories of invisible spirits daily, they will become unable to differentiate the truth or falsity of the stories or perceive if the reality is somewhat distorted.

Intellectual power is very useful in preventing a breakdown of a person's integral character. With the power of intelligence, a person would be able to protect their character; it would work as a safety valve preventing the person from nervous collapse.

In this way, when comparing and weighing the two aspects of having knowledge and having a spiritual constitution, the important thing would be to strive to improve one's intellectual power while having a pure heart. This is how I feel. I think it is important to polish your intellect without forgetting to keep purity in your heart.

So how should we approach this matter? This is the next challenge. The ultimate goal in attempting to improve our intellect should be questioned. Why are we trying to improve our intellect? Is it just a hurdle to be jumped for some kind of certification? Or are we seeking intelligence itself as a goal or to foster intellectual evolution? These are questions to be asked.

Knowledge is indeed useful for a variety of tasks. Therefore, I do not believe it is possible to completely deny seeking knowledge as a worthy endeavor. However, if we are not limited to just use knowledge as a means of signaling to others, but instead, if deepening knowledge itself brings pleasure and enables our souls to evolve, then we could say that there is something very pure in such a kind of knowledge. I believe gaining knowledge merely for the sake of passing exams is shallow and has few positive aspects other than training your brain.

If the goal is not just to learn new mental skills, but to gain a broader perspective of life and to be able to make better judgments from greater understanding, then the learning of such knowledge would boost and improve your entire outlook on life.

Consequently, I believe that the genuineness or purity of one's motivation in seeking knowledge is very important. Such purity would in turn ultimately lead us to the wisdom of the universe. There are many different attributes of God or Buddha. There are many ways that God can be expressed: "God is light," "God is love," "God is courage," "God is energy," "God is many other good things." But another aspect of God or Buddha is undoubtedly wisdom.

The Primordial God or Buddha, who created the universe, is extremely wise and full of wisdom. His creation was well-ordered and purposeful. He who achieved this must be very intelligent and full of wisdom. Therefore, I believe that the supreme goal of seeking knowledge is the wisdom of the Primordial Buddha itself. It is because knowledge is the power to help understand the world and improve it. In the end, the utmost, highest point of improving one's knowledge would be the wisdom of the Primordial Buddha.

It can be said that *rojin* is the highest level of spiritual or psychic abilities; it also involves the power of knowledge or intellectual power that serves to make sense of all things. *Rojin* is fundamentally connected to the wisdom of the Primordial Buddha. Perhaps it is about the different aspects of the Primordial Buddha – whether we see Him as the embodiment of a miracle or of wisdom. Besides *rojin*, you might think of many other spiritual abilities, such as spiritual sight, spiritual hearing, and so on, but these are simply examples of miracles. However, as we comprehend His wisdom as to what lies behind such psychic abilities, it is only natural that wisdom is the ultimate power.

Therefore, at the highest attainment of *rojin* exists Buddha's wisdom. The question is whether we can live our lives as if God or Buddha were present, whether it is possible to live in the same way as God or Buddha lives while living in the flesh.

Consequently, it could be said that knowledge or intellectual power that is connected to ultimate wisdom is a key part of *rojin*, the mystical power.

4

Living Happy Days

In the discussion of Buddha's Truth and its study in connection to *rojin*, I would now like to talk about how to live in happiness.

The answer to the question, "What makes a person happy?" could be the same as the answer to the question, "What kind of person is he or she?" or "What is his or her nature?" Questions such as "What is a person like?" or "What is his or her personality like?" could be answered by defining what makes the person happy.

Since ancient times, there have been other definitions, of course. Some people say, "By observing a person's friends, you can tell what kind of a person he or she is," or "Show me your library, and I will tell you your character." However, I believe that by looking at what makes a person happy, we can generally understand the person's stature, character, life, and spiritual capacity.

For me personally, the greatest happiness is to attain a deeper level of Buddha's Truth, which heightens my level of comprehension. That, in turn, would provide me with a deeper understanding of the world, with a broader recognition of things. This is my personal definition.

Besides my personal perspective, I am very pleased that I can contribute to the creation of greater happiness for many people through the knowledge of Buddha's Truth and His divine plan.

When talking about what makes people happy in this world, I think that very few individuals would say, "The more joy I can create and bring to people, the happier I would become." Yet, making oneself happy only for one's own joy is ephemeral. On the other hand, if a person lives in a way that leads to the happiness of many people, the amount of happiness that comes back to that person will be unlimited. There is a saying, "If you want to be happy, you must be kind to others." This is quite true. If you do things that make others happier, you will naturally be happy.

Of course, I think it is important not to put too much emphasis on the aspect of self-sacrifice. The idea of "sacrificing oneself to make others happy" would probably cause one to have somber feelings. Instead, I believe that choosing the path of "making yourself happy while making others happier" is the way to have truly happy lives.

With these considerations, I would like to return to the idea of happiness in life. In a final measure, it would be important to ask yourself, "Has there been daily progress for my soul? Have I felt the joy of improvement for my soul every day?"

I also believe that true happiness is having the utmost satisfaction that your soul is improving and broadening when other people have been helped to experience joy. It would be important that your soul is joyful as you spiritually advance, that you have expanded to become a greater individual while you take pleasure in observing others being joyful.

Someone once said, "Happiness will escape through your fingers as you pursue it." This could be said of the happiness of the soul. Happiness is something that will eventually be given to you if you live your life intending to provide it for others. But if you chase after it only for yourself, it will eventually fly away like a butterfly.

Thus, I believe that the essence of happiness and the way to be the happiest is to live your life thinking about others, not about yourself. This way of life can make you very happy. It would describe the action of applying *rojin*, the mystical power, to the theory of happiness.

The reason why *rojin* is so important is that it is very closely related to the principles of happiness. This is because people with spiritual abilities, or psychics, tend to be egoists. It is easy for them to become overly proud. It is easy for them to put themselves first because they are acting according to the big-fish-little-pond effect.

Psychics tend to overvalue themselves and think that people around them should just kneel at their feet. However, I am now trying to tell you that this is a mistake. People with such psychic abilities that are only used for expanding and developing their own egos are very fragile and living in precarious situations. Rather, if you are gifted with such spiritual abilities, it is important to consider how to use your abilities for the benefit of as many people as possible.

In this way, efforts to use your spiritual abilities for the benefit of others will return to you in the form of your own happiness. When you strive to use your spiritual abilities to make others happier, your intellectual power will be of great importance.

If your intellectual power is weak, your benevolence may be taken advantage of by the devil, and your good intentions may turn into bad outcomes. This is what can happen.

Therefore, if you want to live a truly happy life, it is important to know how to apply your spiritual abilities in the earthly world.

5

Interest in High Spirits

For one of the topics of this chapter, "Buddha's Truth and Its Study," I would like to discuss the interest in high spirits.

In addition to this book, I have revealed the words of high spirits in various other books. Sometimes I call them spiritual messages, or at times spiritual guidance, or yet sometimes spiritual revelations, but in essence, they are similar in that I disclose communication from the realm of high spirits.

So why do I do this? I would like to talk about this point.

I have made known my communications with Jesus Christ, Moses, and other high spirits, but I have never done this to purposely demonstrate my abilities. I do all this so that many of my readers will know the real essence of high spirits. The reason I share these messages is to make people aware of the different ideals they may want to follow. This viewpoint is important.

People want to have role models to follow, someone who would teach them. People are mortal and have their limitations; no one is perfect. No one has an absolutely perfect character, nor has anyone ever lived a perfect life. However, in the other world, there are spirits who are really very close to God or Buddha. These high-level divine spirits send out brilliant light from their souls, having severed themselves from worldly temptations and desires.

Eventually, our goal is to reach beyond the third-dimensional world, this earthly world, to approach the level of high spirits while still constrained by our bodies and the material world. This is, after all, the secret of how to improve our lives and the source of happiness.

The reason why I have introduced the various revelations of high spirits is that they are truly enjoying happiness. The high spirits are truly happy. They live fully exerting their own individuality, and in total happiness. I believe that the reality of their beings will set great examples for people. There is no high spirit who is unhappy.

I believe that the reason why high spirits have attained such exalted positions is that they enjoy the happiness of being close to God or Buddha. Their happiness is because of their enlightenment; it is the source of their happiness.

I believe that becoming more interested in high spirits will give rise to greater happiness. Even if we study Buddha's Truth, we may not be able to fully understand the thinking of God or Buddha. However, by studying the thinking of those who are closer to God or Buddha, we too can get closer to divinity. I think this is very important.

Therefore, the goal of studying spiritual messages is not just to improve one's intellect, but also to learn the thinking of great souls who were once embodied as people. It would be important to study and understand the high spirits' way of thinking. It is important how well we can assimilate their thoughts and use them to nourish our own souls. A human being has a certain amount of natural knowledge, but we can also gain more understanding by having one or more teachers to learn from.

Self-study is one way of learning, and those who have studied on their own and established themselves in an academic field are certainly to be commended as self-made persons. However, they are respected because they are rare cases.

Most people, about 80% to 90% of them, will make progress by having the right guide, the right teacher. If there were no schools, no teachers, and if children had to acquire knowledge on their own, it would be very difficult, nearly impossible to make progress. It is only when there is someone who teaches effectively that many people can absorb knowledge and pass it on as the legacy of humanity.

If this is the case, then by absorbing the thoughts, feelings, and ideas that the high spirits already possess, by integrating this wisdom as part of ourselves, we would achieve soul evolution. We might be able to add a little more to what the high spirits have learned.

Thus, considering the theme of "Buddha's Truth and Its Study," I would say that having an interest in high spirits is very important. On the other hand, it can be said that the more we become interested in high spirits, the more happiness we can enjoy.

6

A Major Life Goal

In closing this chapter, I would like to make a few remarks about major life goals.

People might be divided into two categories, which are those who have a major life goal and those who do not.

All people have near-term goals. They may be concerned about things like, "How will we make do tomorrow?" "How can we keep to our family budget this month?" "I want to buy a car," or "I have to consider which school to attend by next month."

Being satisfied by only dealing with commonplace goals often indicates that a person is mediocre. Some people, having lived their lives dealing with such small decisions, may spontaneously become great figures, but in most cases, I would say that this is not the case for more than 90% of people.

After all, the reason that a person of great stature is outstanding is that the person had a major goal in life. In reality, children or young adults can have major goals that might lead to potential greatness; however, before long they will usually give up on them.

Why does this happen? Why does one forget one's major goals in life? People most likely would have difficulty maintaining them for long because of a lack of motivation. There would not be enough reason for people to hold onto their aspirations in life. Instead, one would be defeated by reality and fall back. Or perhaps the goal itself was based on one's own egoistic desires. These are questions one has to ask oneself.

Consequently, you should know about certain criteria to be followed when setting a major goal in life. These criteria must be based on the understanding that by studying Buddha's Truth, you become aware of which direction is closer to God or Buddha and set your goals accordingly. Even if you achieve great success in this world, if it causes you to enter the realm of hell when you return to the other world, such success is completely barren of any true value. You could say that such worldly success is meaningless.

Rather, because there can be a great success in this world that would lead to great success in the next world, having it in this world would be meaningful. Basically, I think the most important thing when setting your major goals in life is to eliminate such goals that contradict the mind of God or Buddha.

So what are life goals that do not conform to the goals of God or Buddha, or that go against His mind? Simply put, they would be goals that do not lead to one's spiritual evolution.

In considering this more specifically and concretely, what kind of life goal would lead to spiritual revolution, and what would not lead to it?

First, what does not lead to spiritual evolution? It is materialism, the belief that only physical objects matter over everything else. Despite how deeply you believe in material things, they cannot become a major life goal in the true sense of the word, nor will they lead you to live in accordance with the mind of God or Buddha. The mere desire to possess material things and to put such thoughts above all else must be denied by all means. People who have lived their earthly lives vehemently advocating materialistic beliefs often face severe challenges in the world after death. It is absolutely necessary to awaken to the truth of the soul. Those who have been poisoned by the idea that material things are almighty will inevitably have to reflect on what they have done on earth when they return to the other world. I would like to warn you about this.

So what exactly is it that leads to spiritual evolution? In the end, I think it comes down to practicing love for others. Love is the power that exists between and among people; it is the bond that connects them. It is the power to nurture and improve people. It is about bringing human beings together to multiply each other's strengths. It is the power to make people feel happier; this is love. In the end, having a major goal in life without contributing to love or the progress of love would be in vain. The reason is that God or Buddha is also the embodiment of love. I hope that you choose the kind of life goal that would include acting more for the sake of love.

Yet another point to consider is whether your life goals will have a positive impact on a large number of people. Setting a major goal in life cannot be done without considering that you should influence as many people as possible in the best possible way, or provide the greatest number of people with the greatest happiness or the greatest inspiration. It is important to foster the greatest happiness for the greatest number; it would be "happiness that continues from this world into the next" in accordance with Buddha's Truth.

Thus, in answering what are the major goals of life that would serve spiritual evolution, the first point would be that they must not be based on materialism, only focusing on material things or worldly success. These would set the minimum level of requirements one should follow.

On the other hand, positive requirements would be to contribute to the development of love and to be able to positively influence and inspire most of the people you meet.

Premised on these requirements, let us further consider the question, "What is the major goal of life?" I would say the direct answer is "becoming a person who is closer to God or Buddha." All depends on these words.

"How close to God or Buddha will I become?" "During my life that is only measured in decades, how will I develop a character that is closer to God or Buddha?" "How can I become such a person?" When considering your major goals in life, you would have to answer these questions.

So how should you live your life to become closer to God, closer to Buddha? I believe you should select particular goals for yourself, taking your upbringing, education, thoughts, habits, as well as your character and personality into consideration. These are truly the things you should bear in mind as you live your life on earth.

I believe that the theme of Buddha's Truth and its study is indispensable in helping you find the reason for your existence or to discover your true self to be closer to God or Buddha. Let us continue to make great efforts from now on, paying attention to this theme.

Chapter 6

Serenity Within
and Prayer

1

The Importance of Silence

In this chapter, I will mainly discuss calmness and serenity, or having peace of mind.

First, I would like to talk about the importance of silence. The biggest problem with modern civilization is that we are too busy; there is too much noise around us.

This is a noisy civilization indeed. If music were taken as an analogy to civilization, the playing of jazz or rock music would seem like a harsh disturbance to a person with a quiet mind. I think this is one way to describe modern civilization. The period of classical music is gone, and we are now inundated with music that might be considered hellish, as it lacks the guidance of high spirits (there are exceptions).

The situation is similar for businesspeople. They are so busy. They live with tight schedules having to answer phone calls, messages, and emails in addition to having to receive visitors and attend meetings; they have no time to relax.

This is an age when the value of silence seems to be lost. Occasionally, people might suddenly get the urge to take time off and stroll in one of the historical cities of Kyoto, Nara, or Kamakura. There are times when they feel like resting their minds quietly in those places while gazing at figures of ancient

Buddhist statues. But this would only be for a short while; they would then again merge back into the excited activity of their everyday life.

Unless people are taught, the importance of silence would be hard for them to understand. But occasionally, perhaps once a year or once every few years, people could consider seeking quiet. Suppose a person has a busy job working in a skyscraper in a big city. That person might think that is what people are supposed to do, but may suddenly decide to take time off and find themself standing under the eaves of a mountain temple in Kyoto. They would be surprised at how different it is from the world they are used to.

Settling down in such a quiet place while reading a book or thinking, perhaps staring at a rock garden, the person might ponder over many things during the day. He or she may initially wonder, "What is the value of being human?" or "What is human happiness?" but then mentally wander off. People seem to act on their own accord in these matters, with little guidance.

It is difficult to say which is more valuable to a person's well-being: working busily in a skyscraper in a big city or quietly reflecting on oneself in some retreat or temple. People may tend to seek glamorous lives, but consequently feel that they cannot find homes for their souls in such circumstances. There would be no true peace of mind to be found in doing paperwork or having constant phone conversations.

This realization will intensify when one leaves the earthly world and returns to the other world, the heavenly realm. The excited business activity of this world would only be found in lower levels in the Spirit World.

The higher you go in the spiritual realms, the more harmonious your mind becomes and the more peaceful the surroundings will be. With a background of green mountains and beautiful fields, blooming flowers, dancing butterflies, and flying birds, such circumstances would only engender peaceful conversations. Everyone would be at peace, and the feeling would be as if they were living in eternity.

On the other hand, visiting the lower spiritual realms, you would find the spirits there often busy working as if under time pressure. Of course, the guiding spirits of the higher realms would also be working very hard, but they would always be doing so with a sense of peace in their minds. This is a general comparison of the lower and higher realms.

It can be understood from this that silence is a fundamental desire that lies deep within our hearts and minds. Humans have such a desire for silence within themselves. Why do we seek silence? It is because this is the feeling we once experienced in the home of our souls. There, we once savored the joy that silence gives us.

In a monastery, daily periods of contemplation or silence are observed, when one is not allowed to talk to anyone. The reason for setting aside such time would be to bring back the nostalgic feeling one's soul once experienced when looking within oneself, retrieving one's inner thoughts and feelings through inner conversation.

This is one of the most fundamental human desires. The desire to seek an outward showy display is an expression of one's false self, an external appearance that is not true.

On the other hand, the desire for tranquility aligns with the act of seeking what lies deep within oneself that tends toward God or Buddha. It seems that people today have forgotten the significance and importance of silence.

The practice of a silent lifestyle is a valuable way of life. The busier you are and the more people you meet, the more important it is to set aside time for silence. Then, look within yourself and try to enjoy the pleasures within your heart and mind without being disturbed by various worldly vibrations.

The full enjoyment of the kingdom within and the freedom it gives is eternal happiness that cannot be violated by any person. It is important to secure this eternal happiness.

The busier you are in life, the more you need to take time out to self-reflect in tranquility. It is a time to be quiet, without talking or listening to anything. Five to fifteen minutes of calm time would be enough. Even with such short pauses, the human soul would enjoy spiritual moments. I believe we should not forget such spiritual moments.

2

The Even Road

In a way, observing days of silence can be like traveling on an even road. There are times when people want to do things that make themselves stand out. They may seek prestige in worldly matters, such as trying to gain status, honor, or money.

In some ways, status and honor in this world can be useful to foster the evolution of one's soul. One may be able to experience a wider range of spiritual disciplines due to one's higher standing in society. One may be able to influence many others.

However, if status or honor causes one's mind to waver, the tranquility within will eventually be lost. This would be the reason why people who have only sought worldly status and honor often have miserable lives after retirement in their later years.

It is important to always remain unaltered within, no matter what position or title you attain nor how much money you make. It is important to always have a calm mind like a crystal-clear lake. Always maintain serenity in your mind like a lake abundantly filled with water or the flat sea of spring.

This kind of effort may sound quite mundane and ordinary. However, it is the way to finally become victorious in life.

I believe that no matter what the case may be, whether your activities are the center of attention or you live in the shadows, you must always keep an internal sense of serenity. It should be like the quiet beauty of a calm lake reflecting light like a mirror. The more sensational your lives may be, the more emotional excitement you may experience, but it is also important to maintain an even keel in life.

The following is a parable. There were two monks who, when approaching a riverbank, came across a woman in dismay. She was a beautiful young woman who was troubled because she could not cross the river.

One of the monks thought to himself, "Women are an obstacle to enlightenment, so I must not talk to her. Of course, I must not have physical contact with her."

The other monk came near the woman and said, "If you want to cross the river, I can get you across. Please hold on to my shoulders." He quickly had the woman get on his back and waded into the river. The water came up to his waist as he crossed, but he eventually reached the other side and came out of the river.

The first monk, seeing this, was appalled and indignant, but followed them across the river. The monk carrying the woman set her down on the opposite riverbank, saying, "Well, take care of yourself," and walked away as if nothing had happened.

When the cautious monk caught up with him later, he grabbed the helpful monk by the shoulders and reproached him, claiming, "You have corrupted yourself. You know that part of Buddhist discipline is no contact with women. What is the matter with you talking with the woman and helping her cross the river on your back?"

The other monk replied, "I no longer carry the woman on my back. I didn't know you still do."

This shows an example of people who are bound by rigid thinking; they tend to believe that they can live peacefully as long as they conform to certain rules that prohibit contact with certain people and activities, strictly observing religious precepts but not doing anything else. However, the path of spiritual discipline is not like that. It is not a basic principle of Buddhist discipline to say, "I'm a monk, so I cannot help a woman even if she is in trouble."

When people are in trouble, you should simply help them. It would be ridiculous to be obsessed with precepts even when the person in trouble happens to be a woman. "No matter if it is a woman, help should be provided if possible, then forget the incident when it is over and move on." This is a state of being non-attached.

Even though the precept-abiding monk did not carry the woman on his back, he could not stop thinking about her even after crossing the river. That is how attached he was to the woman in his mind. He was actually the one who carried the woman on his back.

As such, an even road does not mean a road where nothing happens. I am not suggesting that you should live your life avoiding all excitement. I am not saying to take your journey on an even road by retreating into the mountains, practicing austerity while standing under a waterfall, or sitting in a cave.

In the course of human life in this world, various incidents will occur. Events will happen. Therefore, it is necessary to deal with these situations, doing what needs to be done. When taking care of such matters, handle them with promptness while remaining undisturbed within, like the unbroken surface of a lake. This would be the state of non-attachment.

In this way, whatever the outcome it is important to immediately regain a sense of calm. You must not continually linger in the past. There are retired people who constantly talk of their former jobs, as in, "I was an executive at the famous company X," or "I was the president of a company," or "I was the general manager."

However, the power was held by the rank or title in the former organization, not the person in the position. Even if the person left the company, the business would not suddenly sink; another person promoted to take over the job could do it just as well. That is what a job is all about. It is work that could be taken over by someone else.

Therefore, you should never assume that your title or position will last forever. You have to be the kind of person who is able to think in a detached manner, asking, "What would I do if I did not have this job?" But people tend to misunderstand this. They are obsessed with past achievements and name recognition. So it is important to regard these things as transient and to remain constant on the path that you value as important day by day.

For some people, getting married is a critical event of their life, one that has major consequences. However, whether one gets married or not, the main thing that matters is to steadily walk the path of life without becoming overly affected.

In the very lengthy process of reincarnation, one's life on earth is just a brief moment. It is seemingly a fleeting moment. It is not of great importance whom you live with, whom you share your life with, or whom you share your problems with.

It is just like the monk who helped the woman across the river. In one moment he is carrying the woman on his back, but moments after he is walking away. He does not interact with her forever. It was important to help the woman when she needed to cross the river, but once they reached the other side, she just got off his back and they went their separate ways.

As such, there is no need to hide yourself away to protect yourself from the troubles of the outside world, from things caused by external factors. While constantly being affected by the world around us, you need to maintain a steady pace just as today has followed yesterday and tomorrow will follow today in the normal sequence of time.

Even if you were appointed head of your department yesterday but are dismissed today, you should be able to accept it without it upsetting your calm. If you are single today but will be married tomorrow, it should not change you drastically.

It is important to let all things that happen to you to pass without disturbing you, but simultaneously absorb these events in your life as lessons for your soul to learn. When you live in this way, the capacity of your soul becomes enlarged without your notice.

To avoid seeing or hearing things along your life path is not a good thing. It is not enough just to go forward with blinders on like a workhorse. Without the blinders, you could view all manner of things, but you should be content to constantly keep to the path.

When you possess such a state of mind, you will be less obsessed with attachment and stay away from many kinds of confusion. Having a state of non-attachment and a willingness to walk an even road will lead you on the path to great success.

3

The Mindset of a Long-Distance Runner

The willingness to walk an even road is, in other words, the way of life of a long-distance runner. There are many ways to look at life. Some people think of life as a 100-meter sprint, while others think of it as a 400-meter run. Yet others might think of it as a 1,500-meter run. There are many ways to look at life, but I believe that life is basically a long-distance run. Life is like a marathon.

In a marathon, the course will take you over many different footpaths, sometimes on rural trails, at other times on paved roads. Sometimes you run uphill, and sometimes you run downhill. It may rain during the race, or you may have to run under the blazing sun. The wind may blow into your face. It may snow or hail while you are running.

Despite all this, it is most important to know how to maintain your strength and be able to run the full course. No matter how fast you run in the first half of the race, if you tire in the second half and become unable to go further, it is over for you. Also, just because you are only expected to finish does not mean you should take it easy and just stroll to the end.

Based on the idea that life can be compared to a marathon, it is important to effectively pace your strength and time to complete the 42.195 kilometers.

This may hold for swimmers, too. In swimming, there are 50-meter or 100-meter swimming events, but the swimming that is similar to life is long-distance swimming. In long-distance swimming, you cannot swim for long unless you let your body float and ride the waves. You cannot keep swimming against the waves; it is important at times to let your body float to preserve energy. When your body gets tired, it is important to reduce your effort in swimming against the water, but instead to use the water, as if the water and you were one.

Long-distance runners in marathons can experience a similar situation. If a runner's leg movements become deliberate and much effort is needed to run, the runner will not last long. It is important to have steady forward movement, sensing only the sound of one's footsteps behind.

Even if you understand these remarks about running a marathon, you may at times be tempted to sprint short distances in your lives. As you go downhill and feel the momentum to gather speed, you may try to continue running faster, but when the ground starts to slope uphill again, you will need to expend more energy to keep the faster pace. This is what happens.

Therefore, it is important that you not over-exert yourself nor be too relaxed at any given point, saving your strength for the long run. You need to make sure not to become exhausted midway through, but have enough energy left for the final spurt.

The same would apply to your life, after all. The ultimate goal should be to complete running the race. It is most important to keep on running until reaching the end, taking full responsibility for your life and making it something you are satisfied with. No matter how many decades it might last, make your life a satisfying one.

The next consideration is how to allocate your time and energy for complete fulfillment in your life. The question is how you would apportion your time and energy for each of your activities.

In the first part of the race, it would be important to accustom your body to the running pace. As you do so, get a measure of your condition to determine how fast you could run without becoming short of breath.

You could gradually quicken your pace, asking yourself, "Where am I in the whole group? Am I in the lead pack or the second pack of runners?" Find out which group you could keep up with, and do so for as long as you can.

Then, if you spot someone who seems appropriate to follow, try to keep pace with that person. Following a pacemaker would help you keep tempo. At some point, this person may drop out of the race. In that case, you should overtake the person and keep running.

Therefore, it is important to establish a pace in order to conserve your time and energy to complete the 42 kilometers. Please, do not think of life as a short-distance sprint. You need to think of life as a long-distance race and have the mindset of a long-distance runner. If you are preoccupied with winning a race in the short term, it means you are impatient. Even if you cannot expect immediate results, it is important to live in a way that would bring good results in the future.

This is not only relevant when running a marathon; it can be applied to one's working life. When people are seen to be eager for quick advancement up the corporate ranks, there is a reluctance to promote such a person. On the other hand, another person working quietly and selflessly can be seen as more promotable. Such cases really occur. Those who want to show off tend to be shunned by others, while those who work quietly and steadily will be respected.

In this way, having a long-distance runner's mindset is ultimately the path to victory. Continue on a steady pace as you reflect on yourself. You will not have time to think about anything if you run all out for a short distance. However, during a long-distance run, you can think about many things; remember to be self-reflective and run at a constant pace.

Another important thing to remember for a long-distance runner is that you have to train yourself every day. Many people may be able to run 100 meters or so without any preparation. When it comes to running a marathon, however, you cannot suddenly decide to run. It can only be done after training by running a number of kilometers every day. Initially, you would run shorter distances, then gradually increase the distance to longer runs. It is important to strengthen your legs on a daily basis. You have to train not only for physical stamina but also for your mental strength.

Even if you are presently employed, it is important to be a person with skills to be able to survive without your current position, someone who can survive in another environment or be able to take on an even higher position.

You can apply the marathon analogy to work life; if you want to eventually become company president, you must first strengthen yourself as a regular employee so that you can better handle trouble when you take a supervisory role.

When you are a supervisor, you should perform in such a way that you can become the head of the department. As a department head, you should be prepared to become a board member. When you are on the board of directors, then you should be prepared to assume the responsibility of the president. I am trying to explain the mindset for long-distance runners that would cultivate their progress on a step-by-step basis, not one for short-distance runners or quick advancement.

Some people may suddenly reveal their abilities after being promoted, but this does not usually happen. Abilities would be apparent beforehand as the result of the constant buildup of one's strengths. If a person already has the abilities and demeanor of a head of department while working as a supervisor, that person would naturally have a greater tendency to become a head of department. If you show ordinary performance as a supervisor and think, "I'll do my best only when I get promoted to the head of department," the position will not be made available to you so easily.

This also holds true in religious organizations. Some people may think, "If I'm appointed to be a leader, then I'll show my strength," but this does not happen. Conversely, the path of advancement will often open up before you as you continue to increase your strength day by day, to improve yourself day by day. Studying just to get a job or training yourself because the job requires it would not be the right path to follow. I hope my readers will learn the mindset of a long-distance runner.

4

The Nature of Prayer

Next, I would like to talk about the nature of prayer.

Prayer is found in many different religions. Of course, some religions do not practice prayer. Actually, Buddhism does not usually teach about prayer. There is the concept of prayer rituals, but Buddhists do not usually talk about saying prayers.

What is the essence of prayer? What constitutes a prayer? How did prayer come to be practiced? I would like to consider these questions.

Let us consider the case of a long-distance runner before a marathon. The runner's first prayer would be, "Please let me finish the 42 kilometers. Let me be able to continue to run to the end." When one actually begins one's run from the starting line, the runner will probably say, "As I run, please do not let me fall behind others, and let me run in a satisfactory manner."

Facing difficulty at the 10-km or 20-km marker on the course, the runner could say, "Please take away this pain. Let me have the stamina to run to the end of the race without getting exhausted or losing heart."

When the runner reaches the 30-km or 40-km point, the prayer may be, "Let me be able to make the last spurt, allow me to complete my final effort."

When the runner is about to reach the goal, the prayer may be, "Let me reach the goal successfully," and when the goal is crossed, it could be, "Thank you very much for your help all along the race."

In this way, the content of prayer is likely to change depending on the point in time one is experiencing.

All things considered, the nature of prayer is basically "devotion to something other than oneself," or "devotion to something beyond oneself." I believe this is already understood in the nature of prayer.

Why do we feel the need to devote ourselves to something that is beyond ourselves, or leave matters to such a being? It would be because of our awareness that we are part of the great universe created by the Primordial Buddha, that we are also part of a greater life, although we do not know what the future holds as it is a closed book.

Because you are a part of a greater life, you have something within you that connects you to the Primordial Buddha of the universe. When you seek what is within you, you will find what leads to the great God or Buddha. I believe that prayer is a way to invoke that which would lead to Him.

Prayer is never about being conceited, boastful, or self-centered. It is never about giving in to ego-driven desires.

Prayer can be expressed as a ritual to bring out what is originally within us; it is an attribute of God or Buddha. You could say that it is a ritual to call on the infinite power, infinite energy.

I would like to explain that there are certain things you should pay special attention to when you pray. Namely, you are not really looking for power outside of yourself. Prayer is really an attempt to communicate from that which is within you to that which is beyond you. Prayer is the act of discovering what is inside of you and trying to reach something beyond yourself.

Prayer could be explained as communication with those who, from a psychic point of view, could be called high spirits, gods, or Buddha. However, they are not completely separate from you but are beings with whom you have a connection in your soul.

At the time of prayer, there are techniques, means, and methods that are important. They would ensure that one is as selfless as possible.

The communication pipeline leading to the other world can easily become obstructed because those who live in this world have harmful inclinations, such as a desire to control, possessiveness, hunger for power and money, and carnal desire. When people on earth live at the mercy of these desires, this pipeline becomes blocked.

In order to keep the pipeline open at all times, you need to live peacefully with a mind of non-attachment. It would be important to live as if nothing could disturb you, no matter what happened.

Prayer requires you to recognize that what is within yourself is connected to transcendental consciousness. You need to keep the pipeline that leads to transcendental consciousness clear so that it does not become congested. This recognition is essential. Prayers that are superficial and without sincerity or prayers that amplify ego and greed are prayers that lead to the realm of demons; you always need to be careful about how they are said.

I believe that what is important in prayer is to have an attitude of non-attachment, which is like putting total trust in whatever the outcome will be. When a prayer is for self-actualization that is aimed to bring benefit only to oneself, then the prayer may steer in an undesired direction. Prayers like this may lead to the realm of mountain hermits or the realm of *tengu*, who pursue power to force their will over others; they may even lead to the realm of hell. Therefore, it is important to carefully look at the direction of prayers and what their effect will be.

In other words, you must make sure to always pray for the good. Pray for what is good, not only for yourself, but for others, for the world, and society as well. When you pray, examine your heart and mind to make sure there is no taint. Pray with a cheerful heart.

In a sense, it is a dialogue with God or Buddha. It can be said that talking to God or Buddha is prayer. Above all, I would like you to place special emphasis on humility and non-attachment in your prayers.

From another perspective, this spirit of total compliance to how a prayer is answered may almost seem like surrendering your will, but the important thing is not to pray to gain great personal benefit like an easy windfall but to entrust the outcome to God or Buddha while constantly making an effort to improve yourself. Constantly improving yourself is a prerequisite for a prayer to be answered.

If you make no special commitment and say a prayer like, "God, or Buddha, please answer me. If you answer me, I will believe in you. If you don't, I won't believe in you," it would not be a truthful prayer.

As you make constant efforts to become closer to Him, if your prayers could be worded like, "God, or Buddha, if it is your will, please make this prayer into reality," "May you answer my prayer when it is most appropriate," or "If this prayer is not useful for the improvement of my soul, please, God, or Buddha, instruct me how to be better when you will." I think it is important to show submissiveness in a prayer request.

Therefore, for true prayer to be answered, it is important to always have an attitude of humility and selflessness while trying to do better. It is only with this outlook that your total faith can be displayed. It would not be a demonstration of your total entrustment if you pray for your own desires to come true; it would be abandoning any effort that makes you deserve the prayer. Please keep this in mind.

There are many great spirits in the higher realms of the divine world, and they are engaged in various activities. They have greater cognitive ability than people on earth, so they would comprehend much more than humans. Since they have higher-level abilities, they could naturally make available the right thing to the right person at the right time. But the appropriate timing or circumstances do not have to be limited to what the human mind could imagine.

Let us take an example of marriage as a way of self-fulfillment and assume a person prays to be married. If the prayer is based on a pure heart: "I will make myself more useful to society and other people when I get married," then you could think it was a rightful prayer.

However, what happens if, for example, you have a specific person in mind and you say, "Please let me marry that person, by whatever means," and you continue to make this prayer request? If it is a person with whom you might have a divine connection, your prayer will be answered as a rightful prayer. But on the contrary, if you attempt to realize a false prayer through the forcefulness of your will, it would be a selfish and egoistic prayer for self-gratification, aiming to bind the other person to do what you want.

Therefore, this kind of prayer would lead to either the *tengu* or mountain hermit realms, if not hell.

It is a mistake to think that you can freely control others using prayer or the power of your will; this should never be attempted. When saying a prayer, it should not be to constrain or to force anyone to act, but use words like, "If it is your will, may you realize my prayer." You should not measure outcomes of divine arrangement based on the limitations of your ideas.

Pray humbly, saying, "If this person is approved, please let me marry him or her. But if not, then I'll leave it to divine intent. If there is anyone who is a match for me, please let me meet this person. If the time hasn't come yet, I'll wait until the appropriate time."

It is important to pray humbly. If a prayer is intended to force another person to your will at the best time for you and in the way you want, then it is completely wrong. I want to draw your attention to this point.

5

Peace of Mind

After speaking about the nature of prayer, I would now like to say that praying excessively day in and day out may be detrimental to your peace of mind. It can become an obsession.

There is no end to the number of things people might wish for, but most of us do not have so many at one time. Usually, there is one wish that is strongest, followed by a few secondary wishes. When one prays for their strongest wish day and night, it tends to become an obsession and causes harm to one's peace of mind.

In this sense, it is fine to pray for what one desires from time to time, instead of praying for them every day. I would instead rather encourage you to offer prayers of gratitude to God or Buddha daily. Humble prayers should be something like, "Thank you for your guidance. Thank you for keeping me alive every day. Thank you for letting me witness another day," and occasionally say a prayer for the fulfillment of your own self-realization.

If your daily prayer is, "Please make my wishes come true, exactly as I wish," it would be the same as begging for rain. The high spirits in the heavenly realm have to hear a great volume of such voices every day. Even if you say, "Please let it rain, please bring rain for me," it may not be the right time.

Therefore, you should not pray too much, day in and day out, to realize your desires. It is good to do so once in a while, but it is usually recommended that you say a prayer to offer gratitude.

A prayer of thanks is not a request for something; rather, it is the acknowledgment of a favor that has already been given. The fact that you are living a healthy life is a miracle in itself. To live a healthy and happy life is already a miracle. The existence of a miracle does not necessarily change anything. The present moment is a miracle.

It is a miracle that you are quite healthy and happily living with so many people who love you. If those circumstances describe your situation, it is important to be thankful for them. Gratitude is essential. Once you have discovered that you are living thanks to the kindness of many people, you should remember to be grateful to God or Buddha, the source of everything. When you remember to pray in this way, you will find great peace in your heart and mind.

High spirits give service without compensation. They do not receive anything but try their best to live for the happiness of people on earth. So do our guardian spirits. With single-mindedness, they are in charge of people on earth, protecting them without expecting anything in return. You should have a great appreciation for these spirits.

If you thank someone and lower your head to express gratitude, it does not lower your status or your value. By being grateful, human beings can grow even further. You need to realize that this attitude has such a great value.

In this way, continuing your focus on prayers of gratitude will bring you peace of mind and allow you to receive the consideration, happiness, and light of God or Buddha. If you would like to know if you are praying in the right way, just check to see if you are experiencing peace in your heart and mind. If you are peaceful within, your prayers have been right prayers.

On the other hand, if you pray with a heart full of worries, pain, jealousy, suspicion, anger, envy, or resentment, you must realize that your prayers will not be heard in heaven. No matter how formally or beautifully your prayer is worded, it would be in vain for you to ask for your earthly desires to be fulfilled. It would not reach heaven, and even if it did, it would not be heard.

I would like to stress, "Always remember to maintain peace of mind."

6

The Path to Great Harmony

This is the last section of the chapter. I have discussed many subjects, but in essence, I have taught the path to great harmony in the discussion of *rojin*, the mystical power. I have explained what great harmony is, and the path to great harmony.

People easily forget about the spiritual world, becoming content just living in the earthly realm. Naturally, they forget about the spiritual perspective in understanding the world and human life. To keep people from forgetting about their divine connection, at times those with spiritual gifts, like psychics or guiding spirits of light, appear in this world and perform various kinds of miracles.

However, when dealing with miraculous phenomena, people may become so involved with them that these phenomena could cause their downfall. They can become obsessed with miracles, glorifying psychic powers and seeking only to amplify their own desires, but they live their lives at the mercy of the winds of fate.

The important thing to bear in mind is to live a wonderful life in a worldly sense while working toward proving the true world, the real world. What does it mean to live a wonderful life while living in this world? In short, it is to live your life while maintaining harmony within your heart and mind.

Having spiritual abilities while also achieving worldly success can be considered wonderful, but it does not necessarily equate to social status or title while having spiritual abilities. Nor does it mean to build wealth while having spiritual abilities.

The path to great harmony is never about seeking external success, but about living in a way that is approved by God or Buddha. Even if you are gifted with special abilities, you should not be conceited or assume a self-deprecating attitude. Rather, seek to achieve greater human perfection. The path to great harmony is about pursuing a broader mind, a more generous mind, a more tolerant mind, a more diversity-oriented mind, a more excellent mind, a gentler mind, a calmer mind, a more praiseworthy mind; it is to have a mind that is more filled with light.

Having higher social status or becoming a top leader, for example, may come as a result. So might having a greater income. Think of these matters only as results, not causes. Think of them as outcomes, not goals.

In this sense, the ultimate attainment of *rojin*, the mystical power, can be found in seeking great harmony within yourself and pursuing the great harmony of the utopian world; it is achieved through encounters with many people to further your self-discipline and self-refinement.

As a method to attain such great harmony, I have explained in this chapter the importance of having serenity within, and the value of prayer that is in accord with the mind of God or Buddha.

If you have feelings of misery, or conceit that causes you much pain in your heart and mind, try to achieve serenity within yourself. If you can keep your mind calm and serene, be thankful to God or Buddha, and offer Him a prayer of thanks. Then, express a wish that is properly aligned with His mind.

There you will find a great path to progress. There you will find the path to great harmony. With this final note, I close this chapter.

Chapter 7

Lecture on *Rojin*,
Buddha's Mystical Power

Lecture given on July 24, 1988
at Happy Science Training Hall, Tokyo

1

What Is *Rojin*?

This book has focused on the theme of *rojin*, the mystical power. It is said to be among the greatest of the divine powers that Shakyamuni Buddha possessed; I have introduced it to you.

Until now, there has never been any literature that delved so deeply into this subject, nor any materials in this world that have covered discussions of *rojin*. This is a book based solely on things that I have experienced personally and spiritually.

The subtitle of this book is *Its Ultimate Attainment in Today's World* because I believe there is a critical need for the application of *rojin* abilities in current society. Nowadays, various forms of spiritual and psychic abilities are widely talked about; therefore, how *rojin* from Shakyamuni Buddha's time can be applied today should be of interest to people.

First of all, I would like to discuss why *rojin* is needed.

As mentioned in the previous chapters, there are various forms of spiritual abilities, such as spiritual sight, spiritual speech, spiritual hearing, *tashin* or the ability to read the minds of others, foresight, and astral projection. *Rojin* is actually based on these abilities and further serves to cap them off, so to speak. These various spiritual or psychic abilities are useful tools in themselves, but unfortunately, they can be like double-edged swords. This means if they are used in the wrong way, they can not only hurt the user but also those around the user.

For this reason, the ability to be in complete control of each of these spiritual abilities is required.

The spiritual ability of *rojin* involves two aspects:

The first is the ability to determine which ability to use in the range of various spiritual abilities and perform it. It is the power to organize different spiritual abilities, choosing which to use and regulating the intensity and the manner in which each is used.

The second aspect of *rojin* is that it is the greatest methodology for humans to implement, in this world on earth, the thoughts and capacities of action that both originally belong to the other world.

Happy Science aims to create a utopia on earth based on Buddha's Truth, which I teach, referring to the messages and guidance of high spirits. In order to achieve this goal, there is a need for a theory to bridge laws from the spiritual realm to the laws of the world on earth, while fully recognizing the difference between them. This theory of bridging them is actually an implication of the mystical power of *rojin*.

I have been using the ancient term, *rojin*, which is not commonly used today, but if I were to express it differently, it could be called a bridging ability. In modern terms, it is the ability to bridge the gap between the real world and the phenomena occurring in the earthly world.

2

Applying *Rojin* to Earthly Reality

I have just described *rojin* as the ability to bridge the gap between the real world and the phenomena occurring in this world.

Now, I would like to discuss the issues and challenges when applying *rojin* to earthly reality. Three possible issues may be expected when *rojin* is combined with earthly happenings.

1) Reconciling what is sensed of the spiritual world with what is sensed by the physical body

The first is the question of how to reconcile things sensed of the spiritual world with the five senses used to determine reality in this world.

For example, if you have spiritual sight, you can perceive the attributes of various spirits. You will be able to see their auras and sense the spiritual atmosphere surrounding them as well as their spiritual form. When these otherworldly senses are particularly developed, they can cause a considerable disturbance to one's regular physical senses.

So, how can one overcome this? This is an important question, and the answer is to build a solid basis of spiritual knowledge.

The reason you become uneasy when seeing various spiritual phenomena is that they seem strange and shocking; they are beyond your familiar experience.

Therefore, the first positive step is to be able to understand the presence of spiritual phenomena in a way that you can explain them to yourself. If you are able to see spirits or hear voices, it is important to be able to explain the phenomena in a way that can immediately make sense to you.

If you are unable to explain them or do not have sufficient spiritual knowledge, it could be rather upsetting when seeing a ghost in a graveyard or one appearing by your bedside in the middle of the night, for example. But once you know the truth of the spiritual world, you will not be disturbed when you see a ghost. It will be no mystery to you.

Moreover, you would instantly see why these spirits were in the state they were in. By studying further, you would be able to see what is wrong with their minds, and what mistakes they made. When encountering a ghost, you would instantly ascertain its mistakes and know what to say to it. There is nothing to be afraid of, even if you can see such spiritual figures.

Therefore, I want to state that the first requirement in applying the mystical power of *rojin* to real-life occurrences is to enhance your spiritual knowledge and knowledge of Buddha's Truth.

2) When the timeliness of supernatural insight causes a mismatch with earthly time

A second issue emerges when the mystical power of *rojin* is combined with earthly reality: One's insight begins to act supernaturally.

This refers to insight into the essence of things. It is the ability to take in the essence of things and gain a deep understanding. With this ability, one can understand such things as what other people are thinking, the core elements of the things one does at work, or what the conclusion will be as soon as one joins in a meeting.

A problem could arise because of the gap between earthly time and time that is perceived with spiritual intuition. For those living on earth, time seems to flow very slowly, much like a glacier moves at an extremely slow pace. On the other hand, people with the relevant spiritual abilities would be able to understand things right away because of their spiritual intuition. Such intuition is subject to guidance from the realm of high spirits.

For a person who can foresee outcomes, how would the earthly world appear? It would seem very strange, as if all movement were in slow motion.

Therefore, events that are related to or are a result of this second issue should be handled with an additional perspective, that is, the ability to know how others feel.

It is not enough to consider one's own feelings. Other people without spiritual abilities cannot share the feelings or quickly reach the same conclusion as one with greater intuition. Therefore, it is necessary to recognize that more time would be required for others to reach the same conclusion and that more explanation would be needed.

This is actually closely related to the ability to teach Truth in a personalized manner, in accordance with each person's capacity and circumstances.

If an enlightened person tries to explain his or her own enlightenment to other people in a manner that is too hasty, it will be difficult for the listeners to understand, and it could cause problems to arise in the process of conveying the Truth.

This problem is not only relevant to believers today. When Shakyamuni Buddha began his missionary work more than 2,500 years ago, he once stumbled on this same issue.

When he tried to hurriedly explain his enlightenment to others, he was not able to instill the ideas of his teachings for them to become believers.

This is exactly the point when the ability to teach people in a way that best suits them becomes necessary. It is about understanding how other people feel. You need to judge how you look from the perspective of others, not your own. If this is not achieved, the mystical power of *rojin* will not be accomplished.

3) How to reconcile the longing for the spiritual world with earthly reality

The third issue to address when applying *rojin* to earthly circumstances is how to reconcile the longing for the spiritual world with daily life.

After acquiring advanced psychic abilities and having regular conversations with spiritual beings, one's view of life would inevitably become more otherworldly. Then, there would naturally be a yearning for the real world beyond this world on earth.

Therefore, the third issue is how to find meaning in earthly life while immersed in spiritual awareness.

When your eyes are opened to the spiritual world, it is as if the physical world would instantly fade away. The physical things before you would seem to lose color, like a sepia photograph that has become faint or blurry. The key is how to breathe life into the things that have turned blurry.

What kind of truth is there to discover in this world, rather than becoming a person totally absorbed in the other world? How would one find the light of a soul that would shine brightly in this life on earth, and how would one acquire food for one's heart and mind? These would be important themes to focus on.

Unless this third issue is resolved, *rojin* will never be complete, and even those who can make full use of their spiritual abilities will not be able to fully enjoy happiness in their earthly lives.

Please refer to these three issues when considering the application of *rojin* to earthly matters.

3

Enlightenment and *Rojin*, the Mystical Power

The next question is, "Is there a relationship between what is called enlightenment and *rojin*, the mystical power?

In sum, I would say that *rojin* would fulfill the role of the backbone that supports enlightenment.

People tend to give abstract meanings to the word "enlightenment" and see it as something that is attained with temporary duration.

The same applies to Zen Buddhism, where enlightenment is often referred to as the joy of discovery or the joy of seeing the sparkle of the soul. But unfortunately, such occurrences of enlightenment accompanied with joy have a drawback; they are short-lived. Even though such blissful moments of joy can come at some point in one's life, the sense of happiness gradually fades away. Although one might think that one has attained enlightenment, the content of that enlightenment will gradually erode and become lost.

In truth, *rojin* allows one to fully enjoy the happiness that comes with enlightenment and to continue to enjoy the experience for the rest of one's life. That is why I defined *rojin* as having the functions of the backbone supporting enlightenment. It is only with this backbone that the other physical structures can develop.

In order to experience the joy of enlightenment for a long time, it is necessary to maintain an unwavering self in the face of the constantly changing winds of earthly life. To preserve and maintain the unwavering self, the unshakable self, the self as a child of God or Buddha, and the self that does not drift away in the flow of time, the mystical power *rojin* is required. It is the greatest of all spiritual or psychic abilities, and it involves the power to apply spiritual abilities to earthly life.

As such, *rojin* is not exactly the same as enlightenment. However, I would state with confidence that *rojin* constitutes the core and the backbone of enlightenment; it is an important pillar for building the framework of enlightenment.

4

Rojin and *Kanjizai*

Now, I would like to discuss the next theme, *rojin* and *kanjizai*. In this book, I have previously explained *kanjizai* and intend to write a book on this subject on another occasion.

Let me clarify my views on how *rojin* and *kanjizai* are related, and how they should be understood in the context of current times.

In short, the powers of *kanjizai* and *rojin* can be described as two opposing vectors, outward and inward vectors respectively. At the same time, achieving a balance of these opposing vectors will serve to stabilize one's human qualities.

What does this mean? As one's spiritual or psychic abilities develop and progress, one will achieve a profound understanding of many things. Not only will one understand the feelings of people, but one will also experience various phenomena, such as comprehending the appearance and thoughts of spiritual beings of the other world, seeing the realms that do not exist on earth, recognizing truths about the past, or predicting the future to some extent. Such kinds of experiences can be further deepened.

However, when considering the self, the physical being that exists in this world on earth, if the power of *kanjizai* becomes great, it will cause one to lose balance in one's own personality. Therefore, the more the power of *kanjizai* is enhanced, the stronger the power of *rojin* is required to grow.

Both of these mystical powers share something in common in that they make full use of spiritual or psychic abilities, but they differ in the direction of their application; outward or inward. While *kanjizai* is the power of outward observation, *rojin* has much to do with establishing oneself, knowing how to control one's inner self and how to firmly build one's inner world.

In addition to one's own self-power, other power may play a great role when spiritual abilities are initiated. However, the mystical power of *rojin* can never be achieved through other power alone. *Rojin* is a power that emerges as one establishes and develops oneself.

Therefore, it is important to keep in mind that the more powerful *kanjizai* becomes, the more energy is needed to reinforce oneself.

5

The Main Path of Spiritual Disciplines

As one's spiritual abilities become enhanced, the need for self-improvement and self-establishment becomes indispensable. As the "self" to be established becomes greater and greater, there are more expectations and requirements that come along with it.

To consider the way to fulfill these requirements, some people might consider the path to human perfection as Confucius did. Some may consider Leonardo da Vinci or Emanuel Swedenborg as models. Yet others may think of Plato and Socrates.

In any case, what guidelines do we need to bear in mind? If one recognizes the growth of one's spiritual abilities, the greater this awareness, the more effort is required for one to leave behind achievements and accomplishments that will benefit people in the world.

If the balance between these two factors is not achieved, stability will be lost. The more affirmation you have of the development of your spiritual abilities, the more important it becomes to give back love and greater happiness to society.

Therefore, the more advanced a person is in the practice of Truth, the more grateful he or she should be for being allowed to live and for having been blessed with spiritual gifts, and the more steps he or she should take to give something back to the people of the world.

This act of giving back to the world may be expressed in the form of fine arts, as in the case of da Vinci, or as in Swedenborg's case, in the form of some 150 books on various inventions and discoveries in this world as well as accounts of the spiritual world. As for Plato, his contribution to the world was in the form of systems of philosophical thought. What these individuals all had in common was that they worked hard to pass on what they gained as their intellectual and spiritual heritage to future generations. As they developed their spiritual abilities, they did not indulge in self-satisfaction. It can also be understood that these great figures made efforts to share what they had acquired with their contemporaries through teaching or in other ways; they aimed to give others the opportunity to enjoy their achievements as well.

There is a clear difference between these geniuses and the *tengu*, the long-nosed goblins who boast of the "enlightenment" they claim to have achieved by practicing religious austerity under waterfalls or by undergoing the Thousand-day Circumambulation, the religious discipline of walking on mountainous trails for 1,000 days. The more enlightened you become or the more you develop your spiritual abilities, the more you will have to be a person motivated to give back to others with limitless love.

In case someone lacks this mindset, the development of his or her spiritual abilities must be questioned because it could turn out in an undesirable way.

The development of one's spiritual abilities is not easily confirmed by others. It is only recognizable by examining oneself.

Therefore, you must daily examine yourself in terms of giving back love to the world, and by applying your spiritual abilities in day-to-day life on earth. These can be confirmed by your own perception.

How many people have you made happy? Have you been able to inspire and educate anyone? Were you able to give words of inspiration to those suffering in life and cause them to be saved?

I pose these questions to you. Here, you can find the main path of spiritual disciplines.

AFTERWORD

This book has been compiled to give an overall picture of spiritual or psychic abilities and to serve as a guide for those who are walking the path to enlightenment.

Chapter 1, "A Spiritual View of Life," and Chapter 2, "Theories of Spiritual Phenomena," are introductory, written in a way that beginners can understand. Chapter 3, "Different Kinds of Spiritual Ability," and Chapter 4, "*Rojin*, the Mystical Power," constitute the main sections of the book, and I believe they contain advanced subject material for seekers of Truth. Chapter 5, "Buddha's Truth and Its Study," and Chapter 6, "Serenity Within and Prayer," suggest the practical applications of *rojin*, the mystical power, which I believe are easily understood by the general public.

It is my great pleasure to be able to publish a book about one of the essences of Shakyamuni's Buddhism, making it available to the public in today's world.

Ryuho Okawa
Master & CEO of Happy Science Group
March 1988

ABOUT THE AUTHOR

RYUHO OKAWA was born on July 7th 1956, in Tokushima, Japan. After graduating from the University of Tokyo with a law degree, he joined a Tokyo-based trading house. While working at its New York headquarters, he studied international finance at the Graduate Center of the City University of New York. In 1981, he attained Great Enlightenment and became aware that he is El Cantare with a mission to bring salvation to all humankind. In 1986, he established Happy Science. It now has members in over 160 countries across the world, with more than 700 local branches and temples as well as 10,000 missionary houses around the world. The total number of lectures has exceeded 3,300 (of which more than 150 are in English) and over 2,850 books (of which more than 600 are Spiritual Interview Series) have been published, many of which are translated into 37 languages. Many of the books, including *The Laws of the Sun* have become best sellers or million sellers. To date, Happy Science has produced 23 movies. The original story and original concept were given by the Executive Producer Ryuho Okawa. Recent movie titles are *Beautiful Lure–A Modern Tale of "Painted Skin"* (live-action, May 2021), *Into the Dreams...and Horror Experiences* (live-action movie scheduled to be released in August 2021), and *The Laws of the Universe-The Age of Elohim* (animation movie scheduled to be released in October 2021). He has also composed the lyrics and music of over 450 songs, such as theme songs and featured songs of movies. Moreover, he is the Founder of Happy Science University and Happy Science Academy (Junior and Senior High School), Founder and President of the Happiness Realization Party, Founder and Honorary Headmaster of Happy Science Institute of Government and Management, Founder of IRH Press Co., Ltd., and the Chairperson of NEW STAR PRODUCTION Co., Ltd. and ARI Production Co., Ltd.

WHAT IS EL CANTARE?

El Cantare means "the Light of the Earth," and is the Supreme God of the Earth who has been guiding humankind since the beginning of Genesis. He is whom Jesus called Father and Muhammad called Allah, and is the Creator in Shintoism, *Ame-no-Mioya-Gami*. Different parts of El Cantare's core consciousness have descended to Earth in the past, once as Alpha and another as Elohim. His branch spirits, such as Shakyamuni Buddha and Hermes, have descended to Earth many times and helped to flourish many civilizations. To unite various religions and to integrate various fields of study in order to build a new civilization on Earth, a part of the core consciousness has descended to Earth as Master Ryuho Okawa.

El Cantare,
God of the Earth

| **Ra Mu** | **Alpha** | **Elohim** | **Shakyamuni Buddha** |
| 17,000 years ago | 330 million years ago | 150 million years ago | 2,600 years ago |

Thoth
12,000 years ago

Hermes
4,300 years ago

Rient Arl Croud
7,000 years ago

Ophealis
6,500 years ago

Ryuho Okawa

Alpha is a part of the core consciousness of El Cantare who descended to Earth around 330 million years ago. Alpha preached Earth's Truths to harmonize and unify Earth-born humans and space people who came from other planets.

Elohim is a part of El Cantare's core consciousness who descended to Earth around 150 million years ago. He gave wisdom, mainly on the differences of light and darkness, good and evil.

Shakyamuni Buddha was born as a prince into the Shakya Clan in India around 2,600 years ago. When he was 29 years old, he renounced the world and sought enlightenment. He later attained Great Enlightenment and founded Buddhism.

Hermes is one of the 12 Olympian gods in Greek mythology, but the spiritual Truth is that he taught the teachings of love and progress around 4,300 years ago that became the origin of the current Western civilization. He is a hero that truly existed.

Ophealis was born in Greece around 6,500 years ago and was the leader who took an expedition to as far as Egypt. He is the God of miracles, prosperity, and arts, and is known as Osiris in the Egyptian mythology.

Rient Arl Croud was born as a king of the ancient Incan Empire around 7,000 years ago and taught about the mysteries of the mind. In the heavenly world, he is responsible for the interactions that take place between various planets.

Thoth was an almighty leader who built the golden age of the Atlantic civilization around 12,000 years ago. In the Egyptian mythology, he is known as god Thoth.

Ra Mu was a leader who built the golden age of the civilization of Mu around 17,000 years ago. As a religious leader and a politician, he ruled by uniting religion and politics.

ABOUT HAPPY SCIENCE

Happy Science is a global movement that empowers individuals to find purpose and spiritual happiness and to share that happiness with their families, societies, and the world. With more than 12 million members around the world, Happy Science aims to increase awareness of spiritual truths and expand our capacity for love, compassion, and joy so that together we can create the kind of world we all wish to live in.

Activities at Happy Science are based on the Principles of Happiness (Love, Wisdom, Self-Reflection, and Progress). These principles embrace worldwide philosophies and beliefs, transcending boundaries of culture and religions.

Love teaches us to give ourselves freely without expecting anything in return; it encompasses giving, nurturing, and forgiving.

Wisdom leads us to the insights of spiritual truths, and opens us to the true meaning of life and the will of God (the universe, the highest power, Buddha).

Self-Reflection brings a mindful, nonjudgmental lens to our thoughts and actions to help us find our truest selves—the essence of our souls—and deepen our connection to the highest power. It helps us attain a clean and peaceful mind and leads us to the right life path.

Progress emphasizes the positive, dynamic aspects of our spiritual growth—actions we can take to manifest and spread happiness around the world. It's a path that not only expands our soul growth, but also furthers the collective potential of the world we live in.

PROGRAMS AND EVENTS

The doors of Happy Science are open to all. We offer a variety of programs and events, including self-exploration and self-growth programs, spiritual seminars, meditation and contemplation sessions, study groups, and book events.

Our programs are designed to:
* Deepen your understanding of your purpose and meaning in life
* Improve your relationships and increase your capacity to love unconditionally
* Attain peace of mind, decrease anxiety and stress, and feel positive
* Gain deeper insights and a broader perspective on the world
* Learn how to overcome life's challenges
  ... and much more.

*For more information, visit **happy-science.org**.*

CONTACT INFORMATION

Happy Science is a worldwide organization with faith centers around the globe. For a comprehensive list of centers, visit the worldwide directory at *happy-science.org*. The following are some of the many Happy Science locations:

UNITED STATES AND CANADA

New York
79 Franklin St., New York, NY 10013
Phone: 212-343-7972
Fax: 212-343-7973
Email: ny@happy-science.org
Website: happyscience-usa.org

New Jersey
725 River Rd, #102B, Edgewater, NJ 07020
Phone: 201-313-0127
Fax: 201-313-0120
Email: nj@happy-science.org
Website: happyscience-usa.org

Florida
5208 8th St., St. Zephyrhills, FL 33542
Phone: 813-715-0000
Fax: 813-715-0010
Email: florida@happy-science.org
Website: happyscience-usa.org

Atlanta
1874 Piedmont Ave., NE Suite 360-C
Atlanta, GA 30324
Phone: 404-892-7770
Email: atlanta@happy-science.org
Website: happyscience-usa.org

San Francisco
525 Clinton St.
Redwood City, CA 94062
Phone & Fax: 650-363-2777
Email: sf@happy-science.org
Website: happyscience-usa.org

Los Angeles
1590 E. Del Mar Blvd., Pasadena, CA 91106
Phone: 626-395-7775
Fax: 626-395-7776
Email: la@happy-science.org
Website: happyscience-usa.org

Orange County
10231 Slater Ave., #204
Fountain Valley, CA 92708
Phone: 714-659-1501
Email: oc@happy-science.org
Website: happyscience-usa.org

San Diego
7841 Balboa Ave., Suite #202
San Diego, CA 92111
Phone: 626-395-7775
Fax: 626-395-7776
E-mail: sandiego@happy-science.org
Website: happyscience-usa.org

Hawaii
Phone: 808-591-9772
Fax: 808-591-9776
Email: hi@happy-science.org
Website: happyscience-usa.org

Kauai
3343 Kanakolu Street, Suite 5
Lihue, HI 96766, U.S.A.
Phone: 808-822-7007
Fax: 808-822-6007
Email: kauai-hi@happy-science.org
Website: happyscience-usa.org

Toronto
845 The Queensway
Etobicoke ON M8Z 1N6 Canada
Phone: 1-416-901-3747
Email: toronto@happy-science.org
Website: happy-science.ca

Vancouver
#201-2607 East 49th Avenue
Vancouver, BC, V5S 1J9, Canada
Phone: 1-604-437-7735
Fax: 1-604-437-7764
Email: vancouver@happy-science.org
Website: happy-science.ca

INTERNATIONAL

Tokyo
1-6-7 Togoshi, Shinagawa
Tokyo, 142-0041 Japan
Phone: 81-3-6384-5770
Fax: 81-3-6384-5776
Email: tokyo@happy-science.org
Website: happy-science.org

Seoul
74, Sadang-ro 27-gil,
Dongjak-gu, Seoul, Korea
Phone: 82-2-3478-8777
Fax: 82-2-3478-9777
Email: korea@happy-science.org
Website: happyscience-korea.org

London
3 Margaret St.
London,W1W 8RE United Kingdom
Phone: 44-20-7323-9255
Fax: 44-20-7323-9344
Email: eu@happy-science.org
Website: happyscience-uk.org

Taipei
No. 89, Lane 155, Dunhua N. Road
Songshan District, Taipei City 105, Taiwan
Phone: 886-2-2719-9377
Fax: 886-2-2719-5570
Email: taiwan@happy-science.org
Website: happyscience-tw.org

Sydney
516 Pacific Hwy, Lane Cove North,
NSW 2066, Australia
Phone: 61-2-9411-2877
Fax: 61-2-9411-2822
Email: sydney@happy-science.org

Malaysia
No 22A, Block 2, Jalil Link Jalan Jalil Jaya 2,
Bukit Jalil 57000, Kuala Lumpur, Malaysia
Phone: 60-3-8998-7877
Fax: 60-3-8998-7977
Email: malaysia@happy-science.org
Website: happyscience.org.my

Brazil Headquarters
Rua. Domingos de Morais 1154,
Vila Mariana, Sao Paulo SP
CEP 04010-100, Brazil
Phone: 55-11-5088-3800
Email: sp@happy-science.org
Website: happyscience.com.br

Nepal
Kathmandu Metropolitan City Ward
No. 15,
Ring Road, Kimdol,
Sitapaila Kathmandu, Nepal
Phone: 97-714-272931
Email: nepal@happy-science.org

Jundiai
Rua Congo, 447, Jd. Bonfiglioli
Jundiai-CEP, 13207-340
Phone: 55-11-4587-5952
Email: jundiai@happy-science.org

Uganda
Plot 877 Rubaga Road, Kampala
P.O. Box 34130, Kampala, Uganda
Phone: 256-79-4682-121
Email: uganda@happy-science.org
Website: happyscience-uganda.org

ABOUT HAPPINESS REALIZATION PARTY

The Happiness Realization Party (HRP) was founded in May 2009 by Master Ryuho Okawa as part of the Happy Science Group to offer concrete and proactive solutions to the current issues such as military threats from North Korea and China and the long-term economic recession. HRP aims to implement drastic reforms of the Japanese government, thereby bringing peace and prosperity to Japan. To accomplish this, HRP proposes two key policies:

1) Strengthening the national security and the Japan-U.S. alliance, which plays a vital role in the stability of Asia.

2) Improving the Japanese economy by implementing drastic tax cuts, taking monetary easing measures and creating new major industries.

HRP advocates that Japan should offer a model of a religious nation that allows diverse values and beliefs to coexist, and that contributes to global peace.

*For more information, visit **en.hr-party.jp***

HAPPY SCIENCE ACADEMY
JUNIOR AND SENIOR HIGH SCHOOL

Happy Science Academy Junior and Senior High School is a boarding school founded with the goal of educating the future leaders of the world who can have a big vision, persevere, and take on new challenges.

Currently, there are two campuses in Japan; the Nasu Main Campus in Tochigi Prefecture, founded in 2010, and the Kansai Campus in Shiga Prefecture, founded in 2013.

Nasu Main Campus

Kansai Campus

ABOUT IRH PRESS USA

IRH Press Co., Ltd., based in Tokyo, was founded in 1987 as a publishing division of Happy Science. IRH Press publishes religious and spiritual books, journals, magazines and also operates broadcast and film production enterprises. For more information, visit *okawabooks.com*.

Follow us on:

Facebook: Okawa Books   **Twitter**: Okawa Books

Goodreads: Ryuho Okawa   **Instagram**: OkawaBooks

Pinterest: Okawa Books

NEWSLETTER

To receive book related news, promotions and events, please subscribe to our newsletter below.

https://okawabooks.us11.list-manage.com/subscribe?u=1fc70960eefd92668052ab7f8&id=2fbd8150ef

MEDIA

OKAWA BOOK CLUB

A conversation about Ryuho Okawa's titles, topics ranging from self-help, current affairs, spirituality and religions.

Available at iTunes, Spotify and Amazon Music.

Apple iTunes:

https://podcasts.apple.com/us/podcast/okawa-book-club/id1527893043

Spotify:

https://open.spotify.com/show/09mpgX2iJ6stVm4eBRdo2b

Amazon Music:

https://music.amazon.com/podcasts/7b759f24-ff72-4523-bfee-24f48294998f/Okawa-Book-Club

BOOKS BY RYUHO OKAWA

RYUHO OKAWA'S LAWS SERIES

The Laws Series is an annual volume of books that are mainly comprised of Ryuho Okawa's lectures on various topics that highlight principles and guidelines for the activities of Happy Science every year. *The Laws of the Sun*, the first publication of the laws series, ranked in the annual best-selling list in Japan in 1987. Since then, all of the laws series' titles have ranked in the annual best-selling list for more than two decades, setting socio-cultural trends in Japan and around the world.

The *27th* Laws Series
THE LAWS OF SECRET
AWAKEN TO THIS NEW WORLD AND CHANGE YOUR LIFE

Paperback • 248 pages • $16.95
ISBN: 978-1-942125-81-5

Our physical world coexists with the multi-dimensional spirit world and we are constantly interacting with some kind of spiritual energy, whether positive or negative, without consciously realizing it. This book reveals how our lives are affected by invisible influences, including the spiritual reasons behind influenza, the novel coronavirus infection, and other illnesses.

The new view of the world in this book will inspire you to change your life in a better direction, and to become someone who can give hope and courage to others in this age of confusion.

---

*For a complete list of books, visit **okawabooks.com***

THE TRILOGY

The first three volumes of the Laws Series, *The Laws of the Sun*, *The Golden Laws*, and *The Nine Dimensions* make a trilogy that completes the basic framework of the teachings of God's Truths. *The Laws of the Sun* discusses the structure of God's Laws, *The Golden Laws* expounds on the doctrine of time, and *The Nine Dimensions* reveals the nature of space.

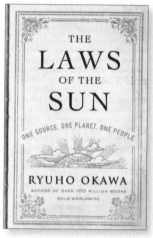

THE LAWS OF THE SUN

ONE SOURCE, ONE PLANET, ONE PEOPLE

Paperback • 288 pages • $15.95
ISBN: 978-1-942125-43-3

IMAGINE IF YOU COULD ASK GOD why He created this world and what spiritual laws He used to shape us—and everything around us. If we could understand His designs and intentions, we could discover what our goals in life should be and whether our actions move us closer to those goals or farther away.

At a young age, a spiritual calling prompted Ryuho Okawa to outline what he innately understood to be universal truths for all humankind. In *The Laws of the Sun*, Okawa outlines these laws of the universe and provides a road map for living one's life with greater purpose and meaning.

In this powerful book, Ryuho Okawa reveals the transcendent nature of consciousness and the secrets of our multidimensional universe and our place in it. By understanding the different stages of love and following the Buddhist Eightfold Path, he believes we can speed up our eternal process of development. *The Laws of the Sun* shows the way to realize true happiness—a happiness that continues from this world through the other.

---

*For a complete list of books, visit **okawabooks.com***

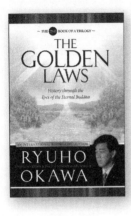

THE GOLDEN LAWS
HISTORY THROUGH THE EYES OF THE ETERNAL BUDDHA

Paperback • 201 pages • $14.95
ISBN: 978-1-941779-81-1

Throughout history, Great Guiding Spirits of Light have been present on Earth in both the East and the West at crucial points in human history to further our spiritual development. *The Golden Laws* reveals how Divine Plan has been unfolding on Earth, and outlines 5,000 years of the secret history of humankind. Once we understand the true course of history, through past, present and into the future, we cannot help but become aware of the significance of our spiritual mission in the present age.

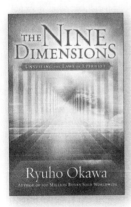

THE NINE DIMENSIONS
UNVEILING THE LAWS OF ETERNITY

Paperback • 168 pages • $15.95
ISBN: 978-0-982698-56-3

This book is a window into the mind of our loving God, who designed this world and the vast, wondrous world of our afterlife as a school with many levels through which our souls learn and grow. When the religions and cultures of the world discover the truth of their common spiritual origin, they will be inspired to accept their differences, come together under faith in God, and build an era of harmony and peaceful progress on Earth.

---

*For a complete list of books, visit **okawabooks.com***

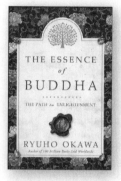

THE ESSENCE OF BUDDHA
THE PATH TO ENLIGHTENMENT

Paperback • 208 pages • $14.95
ISBN: 978-1-942125-06-8

In this book, Ryuho Okawa imparts in simple and accessible language his wisdom about the essence of Shakyamuni Buddha's philosophy of life and enlightenment–teachings that have been inspiring people all over the world for over 2,500 years. By offering a new perspective on core Buddhist thoughts that have long been cloaked in mystique, Okawa brings these teachings to life for modern people. The Essence of Buddha distills a way of life that anyone can practice to achieve a life of self-growth, compassionate living, and true happiness.

THE TRUE EIGHTFOLD PATH
GUIDEPOSTS FOR SELF-INNOVATION

Paperback • 272 pages • $16.95
ISBN: 978-1-942125-80-8

This book explains how we can apply the Eightfold Path, one of the main pillars of Shakyamuni Buddha's teachings, as everyday guideposts in the modern-age to achieve self-innovation to live better and make positive changes in these uncertain times.

THE CHALLENGE OF THE MIND
AN ESSENTIAL GUIDE TO BUDDHA'S TEACHINGS: ZEN, KARMA AND ENLIGHTENMENT

Paperback • 208 pages • $16.95
ISBN: 978-1-942125-45-7

In this book, Ryuho Okawa explains essential Buddhist tenets and how to put them into practice. Enlightenment is not just an abstract idea but one that everyone can experience to some extent. Okawa offers a solid basis of reason and intellectual understanding to Buddhist concepts. By applying these basic principles to our lives, we can direct our minds to higher ideals and create a bright future for ourselves and others.

*For a complete list of books, visit **okawabooks.com***

THE LAWS SERIES

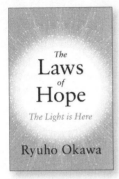

THE LAWS OF HOPE
THE LIGHT IS HERE

Paperback • 224 pages • $16.95
ISBN:978-1-942125-76-1

This book provides ways to bring light and hope to ourselves through our own efforts, even in the midst of sufferings and adversities. Inspired by a wish to bring happiness, success, and hope to humanity, Okawa shows us how to look at and think about our lives and circumstances. By making efforts in your current circumstances, you can fulfill your mission to shed light on yourself and those around you.

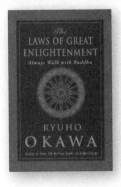

THE LAWS OF GREAT ENLIGHTENMENT
ALWAYS WALK WITH BUDDHA

Paperback • 232 pages • $17.95
ISBN: 978-1-942125-62-4

Constant self-blame for mistakes, setbacks, or failures and feelings of unforgivingness toward others are hard to overcome. Through the power of enlightenment we can learn to forgive ourselves and others, overcome life's problems, and courageously create a brighter future ourselves. This book addresses the core problems of life that people often struggle with and offers advice on how to overcome them based on spiritual truths.

THE LAWS OF HAPPINESS
LOVE, WISDOM, SELF-REFLECTION AND PROGRESS

Paperback • 264 pages • $16.95
ISBN: 978-1-942125-70-9

What is happiness? In this book, Ryuho Okawa explains that happiness is not found outside us; it's found within us, in how we think, how we look at our lives in this world, what we believe in, and how we devote our hearts to the work we do. Even as we go through suffering and unfavorable circumstances, we can always shift our mindset and become happier by simply *giving love* instead of *taking love*.

---

*For a complete list of books, visit **okawabooks.com***

THE LAWS OF SUCCESS
A Spiritual Guide to Turning Your Hopes Into Reality

THE ROYAL ROAD OF LIFE
Beginning Your Path of Inner Peace, Virtue, and a Life of Purpose

THE POWER OF BASICS
Introduction to Modern Zen Life of Calm, Spirituality and Success

TWICEBORN
My Early Thoughts that Revealed My True Mission

WORRY-FREE LIVING
Let Go of Stress and Live in Peace and Happiness

THE REAL EXORCIST
Attain Wisdom to Conquer Evil

THE STRONG MIND
The Art of Building the Inner Strength to Overcome Life's Difficulties

THE HEART OF WORK
10 Keys to Living Your Calling

HEALING FROM WITHIN
Life-Changing Keys to Calm, Spiritual, and Healthy Living

---

*For a complete list of books, visit **okawabooks.com***

MUSIC BY RYUHO OKAWA

THE THUNDER

a composition for repelling the Coronavirus

We have been granted this music from our Lord. It will repel away the novel Coronavirus originated in China. Experience this magnificent powerful music.

Search on YouTube

the thunder coronavirus 🔍   for a short ad!

THE EXORCISM

prayer music for repelling Lost Spirits

Feel the divine vibrations of this Japanese and Western exorcising symphony to banish all evil possessions you suffer from and to purify your space!

Search on YouTube

the exorcism repelling 🔍   for a short ad!

 Available online
Spotify iTunes Amazon

CD available at Happy Science local branches and shoja (temples)